Prison Life
The Crisis Today

Anna Kosof

FRANKLIN WATTS
A Division of Grolier Publishing

New York / London / Hong Kong / Sydney
Danbury, Connecticut

Special thanks to Lawrence Greenfeld and the Bureau of Justice Statistics for their invaluable help in preparing this book.

Dedicated to those who have suffered: the millions of victims, and the people, caught in a tragic cycle, who will never see daylight again.

Photographs copyright ©: Ben Klaffke: pp. 10, 16, 36, 62, 70, 81, 90, 98, 113, 125, 129; The Bettmann Archive: p. 21; Gamma-Liaison/Stephen Ferry: p. 23; Wide World Photos: pp. 29, 55, 102, 116, 118; UPI/Bettmann: pp. 42, 57, 95; Taconic Correctional Facility: p. 48

Library of Congress Cataloging-in-Publication Data

Kosof, Anna.
Prison life: the crisis today / by Anna Kosof.
  p. cm.
Includes bibliograpical references (p.   ) and index.
Summary: Discusses issues such as the youth offender, women in prison, the new challenge posed by AIDS, the impact of drugs, and alternatives to the present system.
ISBN 0-531-10984-4
1. Prisons—United States—Juvenile literature. 2. Prisoners—United States—Juvenile literature. [1. Prisons. 2. Prisoners.] I. Title.
HV9471.K673   1995
365' .6'0973—dc20   95-14886
                                                                  CIP AC

Copyright © 1995 by Anna Kosof
All rights reserved
Printed in the United States of America
6 5 4 3 2 1

Contents

Foreword
by H. Carl McCall
7

Introduction
11

**Chapter One
A Short History of Prison**
19

**Chapter Two
Who Is Incarcerated?**
26

**Chapter Three
The Young Offender**
35

**Chapter Four
Women in Prison**
49

Chapter Five
AIDS: The New Challenge
66

Chapter Six
The Impact of Drugs
78

Chapter Seven
Men in Prison
94

Chapter Eight
Alternatives
107

Chapter Nine
Prison Life Revisited
122

Chapter Ten
Conclusion
131

Notes
136

For Further Reading
140

Index
141

Foreword

Anna Kosof has issued an urgent warning. Ignore it at your peril.

In this searing account of prison life today we learn of a population of young people who are being educated and trained for an unproductive life. We learn of the disastrous waste of human potential and the grave consequences of a self-perpetuating social anarchy. We can no longer afford to ignore these lessons.

A young high school dropout recently provided a frightening commentary on one of the greatest tragedies of contemporary society when he told a reporter, "I hope I get to jail before I turn eighteen. Otherwise I know I'll be dead."

For too many young people, jail or death are the only alternatives. Statistics do not lie. In 1990 the number of prisoners in federal or state correctional institutions reached a record high of 771,243. From 1980 through 1990, the prison population increased by 134 percent.

A growing percentage of these new inmates are young. The number of children under the age of eighteen arrested each year for murder jumped 55 percent in the past decade, to 2,674 in 1990. Juvenile arrests for aggravated assault and forcible rape are also rising dramatically.

Unless we reverse this trend now, we will soon be forced to deal with a multitude of people who have mastered the cold, hard lessons of life behind bars.

Rehabilitation of prisoners is a rarity. Our prisons are overcrowded and understaffed. Drugs and disease are passed from one inmate to another, and the most ambitious corrections officers dream only of maintaining an appearance of order.

It is no surprise that recidivism rates are skyrocketing. Young people leave prison as they entered— unprepared, untrained, and unemployable. All they gain behind bars is a prison record and whatever antisocial skills they may acquire from their fellow inmates. They soon discover that the only financial and personal opportunities available to them are illusory or criminal.

As citizens in a democratic society, we ought to provide young people with an alternative to jail or death. If they are to thrive and succeed, they must have confidence in themselves and hope for the future, and that can come, in part, from education.

The correlation between education and prison is well documented. High school dropouts are three and a half times more likely to be arrested than those who graduate. Nationwide, 83 percent of all prison inmates are school dropouts. Clearly, we must find ways to keep children in the classroom and out of the cellblock.

As Anna Kosof so cogently explains, this task is especially critical for African-Americans and Hispanics. In New York State, 87 percent of prison inmates are people of color. Throughout the United States, nearly one in four African-American men age twenty to twenty-nine is in prison, on probation, or on parole—*more than the total number of African-American men in college.* This is the generation that should be preparing to be the leaders in the twenty-first century.

Anna Kosof teaches all of us. Young readers will benefit from her wise words about the countless advantages of staying in school and resisting the enticement of the fast lane and the quick buck. In these tough economic times, it is more important than ever for young people to hear and believe her message that true opportunity lies in the classroom, not behind prison bars.

It is up to us—and to you as future parents, teachers, and policymakers—to break the cycle of prison, recidivism, and unproductive citizenship. We must assume responsibility for changing the conditions that cause the cycle. We must provide alternatives, and we must insist on rehabilitation and training for those who submit to the destructive forces that surround them.

Our children deserve a future that offers more than jail or death. Pay attention to Anna Kosof.

H. Carl McCall
Comptroller, New York State

Introduction

Entering a prison is one of the most dramatic things you can do. Fear sets in instantly. The sight of the barbed wire, the steel gates, the doors that appear to be permanently shut, scared me, yet I knew that I could leave at the end of the day.

I noticed immediately that each part of the prison was locked and unlocked by an officer. I felt that I was at the mercy of these guards, that I had somehow lost control of my life. And I was a writer, just a visitor. I was treated like a professional, given special privileges, and yet in a prison even an outsider feels the fear of no escape. What if there is a fire? I thought. In prison there is a strange feeling in the air–a feeling that you have lost your freedom. If anything goes wrong, you will be at the mercy of people you don't know, people who have to follow certain rules. You feel totally helpless. And I was not an inmate, sentenced to serve months, years, or a lifetime sentence in prison.

That was my sensation over ten years ago while doing research for *Prison Life in America.* When I returned, to prepare for this book, I wondered what had changed, what had happened to the men and women I had met—some in maximum security facilities, some on death row, some youngsters in drug treatment programs inside the jails.

During those earlier visits many inmates told me sad stories of lives that seemed tragic and led to dead-end roads, of wasted lives. Yet what I witnessed then was not nearly as hopeless as the new crisis the past decade has brought. While we had an increase of inmates back then, we have experienced an explosion since the 1980s. Now the prisoners are younger; many are serving time for drug-related crimes; they are without roots in the law-abiding community. More than on my earlier visits, today's inmates have resigned themselves to spending long periods of their lives in prison. Some will stay forever, and some are dying of AIDS, a disease barely known a decade ago.

Since my last book on prisons, American society has also changed. The number of people living below the poverty level has increased dramatically. In some communities, single mothers are the sole providers in nearly half of the homes. Many are teenagers themselves, unable to properly provide for their children. Millions of people are homeless, and many of them are ex-convicts. Some would rather be in prison than out on the streets without food or shelter. In the 1970s, cuts in funding led to the closing of mental hospitals and the release of countless mentally ill patients. Many more of the mentally ill are now in prison. Other inmates are now infected with H.I.V., the virus that causes AIDS. More women are now a part of the criminal system. Many of them are ill with AIDS, and some have given birth to babies also carrying H.I.V.

In writing the previous book, I felt a sense of tragedy about those serving time, their lost years and tentative future. But now the situation is graver. Now it seems that a generation is serving time without hope and without any real chance of ever finding happiness. They have nothing to look forward to but their release from prison.

In preparing to write this book, I returned to some of the facilities I visited in the past. I interviewed inmates—men, women, youngsters—as well as corrections officers and administrators, and came away with some of the observations that you will read in the following chapters.

In 1993 in the United States, 3.2 percent of the adult population was under the supervision of the Department of Corrections—that is, 5 million persons. According to the U.S. Department of Justice, over two-thirds of these people are on probation or parole; about one-third are in prison or jail. These numbers represent more people than reside in some states. Most of them are men, only 5 percent are women in federal and state facilities. In addition, a disproportionate number of these people are poor and young, have little education, and are repeat offenders. A very large percentage are African-American or Latino, according to the Department of Justice. In 1993–1994, the prison population increased by the record number of 71,000.[1]

Nothing alerts us more urgently to the crisis we face in this country than the sheer number of people who are in the correctional system and the number of crimes they have committed. No government can effectively manage over 5 million people who have been convicted of at least one crime. These criminals are often violent, many have drug or alcohol problems, and many have been in the criminal justice system since their youth. For too many, it's the only address they have ever had. They will spend their entire adult lives without knowing freedom, while living in the world's largest and wealthiest democracy.

The level of crime in this country affects us all. While we may not personally know anyone in prison, we all know someone who is afraid to go out at night, someone whose car has been stolen, someone who is afraid to live alone, someone whose house has been burglarized, or someone who sells drugs. Figures from the National Crime Survey (NCS) show that in 1992, 6.6 million Americans experienced violent acts, and 12.2 million were victims of personal thefts.[2] And many more assaults were never reported to the police. What these figures mean is frightening: the chance of being a victim of a violent crime is greater than that of being hurt in a traffic accident.

These statistics may seem like abstract, remote numbers. But they represent incidents that have created sadness, permanent grief, and trauma in the lives of individuals and families.

Crime rates are counted per population of 100,000 persons. The U.S. homicide rate is 10.5 per 100,000. This means that for every 100,000 people, 10.5 will die as the result of a crime, compared to 2 people per 100,000 in Europe. Thus, an American is five times more likely to be killed than a European. For rape, the U.S. rate is 36 per 100,000, roughly seven times higher than the average in Europe. We are four times more likely to be a victim of robbery— 200 for a population of 100,000, versus 50 per 100,000 people in Europe, according to United Nations data.[3]

In our everyday lives, we are profoundly affected by the over 5 million people in the correctional system. In the 1990s we are spending billions of dollars on prisons. As a result, funding for schools has been reduced. Yet the prison system throughout the country is still estimated to be operating as much as 29 percent over capacity. That means even more money needs to be spent on prison beds, guards, corrections officers, police, and new buildings. All this will cost billions of dollars, and that doesn't include the cost of keeping inmates incarcerated.

From 1980 to 1993, we experienced a 188 percent increase in the state and federal prison population. According to the Bureau of Justice Statistics profile on prisoners, the 1980 prison population was 329,821. That figure jumped to 948,881 thirteen years later, an increase of 619,000 people.[4] The number of additional prisoners by 1994 translates to over 1,500 new prison beds per week nationwide. By the first half of 1994, we had reached a record of more than 1 million men and women serving time in the nation's state and federal prisons. That is *not* people serving time in jail—inmates serving time for a misdemeanor, those waiting for trial or sentencing, or those held for lack of bail—but those *in prison*. These are people who have been caught, and have plea-bargained or been tried by a jury or judge, and were convicted of a crime serious enough to warrant a sentence of over a year in prison.

Why should you be interested in all these people who have committed crimes? Why should you care about people you hope never to meet? Because, unfortunately, they affect all of our lives. These confined people indirectly dictate where we can live safely, with whom we can associate, which parties our parents allow us to attend, how late we can stay out, which neighbors we can speak to, and which parks we can play in.

Too many youngsters cannot go to the park at all because drug pushers and addicts have taken over the swings and slides meant for children. People cannot go out at night because they fear they'll be raped or robbed. Many elderly people are shut in because they feel they can't defend themselves against criminals who may hurt or kill them.

In 1992, a total of more than 33 million victimizations occurred; 23 percent of American households were the victims of crimes, according to the National Crime Victimization Survey (NCVS),[5] which measures crimes such as rape, robbery, aggravated assault, personal theft, burglary, and auto theft. Yes, these numbers are astonishing. We live in a country that has the highest rate of crime and incarceration per person in the world. Why should the largest free country have more people behind bars than half the population of Hungary, or the states of Montana, Oklahoma, and Nebraska combined?

In this book we will take a look inside the prisons and see who lives behind those steel bars. We will examine the severe overcrowding, the spread of AIDS, the astonishing recidivism rate, the overwhelming number of inmates with drug convictions—some of the reasons for the crisis in managing the prison population. We will also look into some of the myths and misconceptions about criminals that prompt government leaders to make decisions aimed at appeasing the public, but which in fact promote racial stereotypes and create unnecessary fear, neither solving the crime problem nor promoting justice.

How can this country continue to compete with other industrial nations when more than 3 percent of its population, instead of being productive, is in trouble with the law? How can we build safe parks and schools when we have to drain our resources to build prisons that will house thousands of inmates?

By 1994, the prison population had swelled to more than a million men and women, many held in the cell blocks of maximum security facilities.

The annual expenditure of the justice system was over $74 billion in 1992. A retired prison official reflected on the relationship between those serving time and the rest of us living outside those tiny cells. "Until we can solve the problems of the ever-growing number of people we must feed, house, and incarcerate, people who only add to the national debt, we cannot solve the other problems in our country."

Too many people are committing crimes and living outside the mainstream of society. Millions of them are unemployed, and many are unemployable; therefore they cannot become productive citizens. Too many people are living in the custody of the state from an early age; too many will never leave prison. And too many are so dangerous to society that we live in fear of becoming their victims.

Why is it that in thirteen short years we have seen such an astounding increase in the prison population? Did the number of crimes increase to such an astonishing level between 1980 and 1993? Or is the government placing greater emphasis and more resources on locking up more people to solve the crime problem? We will look at the recent trends that have changed the criminal justice system, the causes of some of the overcrowding, and our country's response to this social problem. And it *is* society's problem as we are reminded every time a school has no money to buy books, the streets are not cleaned, or the parks and libraries are closed. Some of that money may have been used to keep someone behind bars.

Chapter One

A Short History of Prison

Prison is a relatively recent idea. Sanctions in the ancient world consisted primarily of slavery or indenture to the victim or the victim's family, employment on public-works projects, mutilation or amputation, banishment, or death. There were no trials or sentences as we think of them today. Certainly the concept of long-term confinement as the most common form of punishment is a recent idea. The first court probably appeared around 2000 B.C. for the purposes of settling blood feuds—most commonly, property disagreements.

Interestingly, before the concept of prisons evolved, temples were used for sanctuary—places to which the accused could flee. In those cases where the accused did not manage to find a sanctuary, he or she was punished severely by the accuser; if the crime was serious, death was a common punishment.

The first actual place of confinement for prisoners appeared in the seventh century B.C. when the Greeks constructed underground chambers to hold prisoners awaiting trial. Plato, the Greek philosopher, concerned himself with the issue of crime in the fifth century B.C. He wrote that there should be three prisons: one in the city for persons awaiting trial and sentencing, one for the reform of disorderly persons, and a third, far from the city, for the punishment of felons. In a way, we have the first and the third in the modern-day prison. The place to reform the disorderly—that is, a place for rehabilitation—seems to be the one that many people argue we still need, or need more of.

Throughout ancient and medieval times, people who committed crimes were held in custody in what could be called private prisons. Some people who had power and money built their own prisons and incarcerated those who interfered with their political ambitions. These private prisons were built until about 1800. Crime was not considered the state's problem. Many disputes were handled between the parties involved. The practice of dueling, as a solution to private disputes, continued until the European colonization of America.

The transport of serious offenders to a distant land began in England after 1600. England's first deportation law was passed in 1597. Do you know where these people were sent? Here—to the Americas. When it is said that America was founded by criminals, that's not far from the truth. The British government emptied out its jails and shipped the prisoners over the sea. In the mid-nineteenth century, France and Russia, too, routinely sent their criminals to faraway places. Consequently the need to build prisons for serious offenders was put off.

It was only after the American Revolution that the British stopped sending their felons here. Instead, "convict ships" were put into use. These ships were

In the American colonies, those judged guilty of offenses might be punished by the discomfort and humiliation of the stocks.

equipped with chains, torture devices, and barbaric equipment to put people to death in particularly gruesome ways. Many of the prisoners died at sea. The first prison in America was built in 1773 at Simsbury, Connecticut, about fifty miles north of New Haven. The first inmate escaped eighteen days after he had been sent there. Obviously, it lacked adequate security.

In 1815 New York State established a prison at Auburn. This prison provided for the confinement of inmates at night in individual cells, a regimen of work during the day, and harsh discipline in general. Since maintaining prisons was beginning to be expensive, the prisoners were rented out for various types of work. The authorities reasoned that in this way the prisoners would help pay for their keep rather than be a burden on taxpayers. The prisoners performed hard manual labor, such as working on roads and railways. Many inmates died from beatings, poor food, and overwork.

Most prisons outside the South were built at a time when large industrial facilities were favored. Today these huge prisons, usually located in isolated areas, are still in use. Prisons in the Deep South developed in a different way; to begin with, the buildings were smaller. Mississippi, for example, developed large agricultural operations. The function of these prison farms was known as "work therapy." In Texas and in some other southern states, agriculture is still used as "work therapy."

Today's prisons and correctional institutions are the result of long-term evolution and development. The United States has one of the largest prison populations in the entire world as well as the greatest growth in number of prisoners since 1925 when we started compiling these statistics.

To get an idea of how the prison population reflects society, let's look at the growth rate. From 1925

Prisoners in modern facilities are walled in by advanced electronic security techniques along with barbed wire, fences, and guards.

to 1981, the average yearly growth rate of the U.S. population was 1.2 percent; for the prison population it was 2.4 percent—twice the growth rate of the population at large. The growth rate in the prison population has not been steady since 1925. Between 1925 and 1939 the number of sentenced prisoners grew by 88,000, an average of 5 percent, even though there was virtually no growth in the general population during the depths of the Great Depression, 1932 to 1935. By 1939 the incarceration rate had reached 137 prisoners for every 100,000 people, a level it was not to reach again for forty-one years. Needless to say, general economic conditions greatly affect the crime rate. Whenever a large percentage of people are unemployed, there seems to be an increase in illegal activities and lawlessness.

Wars, too, affect the crime rate. During World War II the prison population decreased by nearly 50,000. Because most of the people in prison are men between eighteen and twenty-nine, the prison population declined when many potential offenders were drafted into the army. During the Vietnam era, between 1961 and 1968, the prison population declined by 30,000. In 1968 the prison population was 188,000, the lowest since the late 1920s. From this point, it grew rather slowly for the next five years. In 1974 it began to rise dramatically and resulted in nearly 150,000 inmates being added. By 1993 the incarceration rate was the highest ever recorded.

So prisons as we know them today are a relatively new concept and the number of people we have in prison and the rate of increase are major problems. Remembering the numbers is not very important, but it is important that you understand that statistical changes in the prison population are a direct reflection of what is occurring outside the prison walls. Wars affect the prison population. The number of young men in a society has a real impact on the rise in prison population. For example, a baby boom, when an unusually large number of people have children, will eventually result in an increase in the number of people who are incarcerated when that generation turns about eighteen. Bad economic conditions and high unemployment also have a great impact on the prison population.

Chapter Two

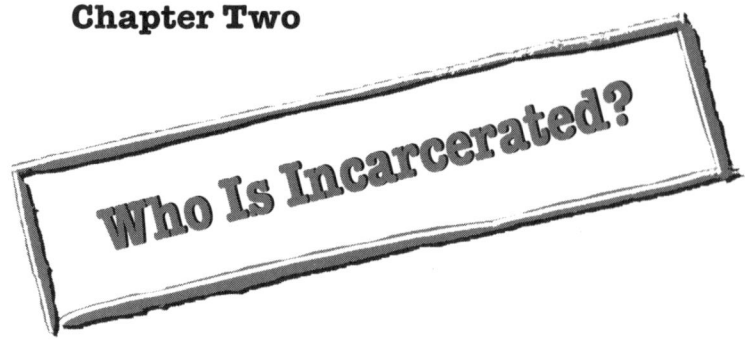

Crime has become fashionable. Journalists exploit sensational crimes and create celebrity criminals. Television programs like "Cops," "America's Most Wanted," "Law and Order," and "NYPD Blue" and many others enter our living rooms and imprint images onto our brains, images that often conjure up fear.

In 1988, when Governor Michael Dukakis ran for president against George Bush, one of Mr. Bush's television advertisements particularly alarmed the nation. It showed an African-American male, Willie Horton, who had been convicted of a homicide that he committed while he was on parole. Over 220 million Americans repeatedly saw the image of a convicted criminal who had been let out of prison on furlough and had then killed an innocent human being.

Many people were alarmed by that image, and the ad may have helped elect George Bush. Four years later President Bush and his staff denounced the ad and admitted that it should have been dropped. But it had been effective. It produced the desired effect: a belief that Michael Dukakis would not be tough on crime.

Crime in this country is an explosive subject. Politicians use it as an issue and play on our fears and emotions. To this situation add the fact that the general public is deeply ignorant about crime, criminals, and the criminal justice system. Politicians present statistics and information to serve their own interests and those of the political organizations they represent. In the end, the public is confused about what to believe and what the facts are in this emotionally charged area.

While looking at the television image of Willie Horton, the criminal who killed while out on furlough, few people stopped to think that a governor has very little to do with paroling a prisoner or giving a convict a weekend pass. Presidential candidates often state their position on capital punishment, but in reality the president does not have a say on whether convicted killers should receive the death penalty. The president's responsibility is to appoint justices to the Supreme Court, subject to Senate approval. Those justices vote in Supreme Court cases that involve capital punishment.

We appear to be tough on crime if we support capital punishment. Yet capital punishment is only one of many criminal justice issues confronting the nation. Between 1976, when the Supreme Court ruled to allow capital punishment for certain crimes, and 1992, only 166 prisoners were put to death. In 1993, ten states executed a total of thirty-eight prisoners, of the more than two thousand under sentence of death. Probably more prisoners will die from AIDS than will be executed. Furthermore, out of the millions of convicted offenders, very few prisoners have committed crimes punishable by the death penalty.

The criminal justice system is in a crisis. It faces a number of desperately serious problems: overcrowding, inadequate funding, old facilities in dire need of repair, a younger prison population serving longer sentences. And these problems are not confined to the nation's prisons. They spill over into all areas of life in our society.

Many people want to know why the nation's prisons are now forced to operate at 18 to 29 percent above capacity. Are more crimes being committed, or have arrests and prison admissions for serious crimes been increasing in the thirty years we have been reporting crime statistics? In other words, is there more crime or are we doing a better job of convicting criminals and keeping them behind bars?

As we saw earlier, the number of prisoners in the United States in 1994 reached a record high of more than 1 million. Compare that figure to 1980, when the number of people incarcerated in federal and state institutions was 329,821, or about one-third of the current figure. This is a 188 percent increase.

So, the number of federal and state prisoners is bigger than ever before, and facilities have not kept pace with the increase. Since 1980 the number of sentenced inmates per 100,000 of the population has risen from 139 to 373. Another aspect of these figures is revealed when we add the next variable: at the end of 1990, women accounted for only 5.7 percent of prisoners nationwide, or 38 per 100,000 females in the resident population. Men are incarcerated at a rate 18 times higher than that for women, or 679 per 100,000 in the resident population.[1]

The number of women under the jurisdiction of state or federal prison officials reached a record high of more than 40,000 at the end of 1991.[2] But the number of women serving time behind bars is still very small in comparison to the number of men.

So far, the figures we have given are for prisons, which are state or federal institutions. While the general public may not differentiate between prisons and

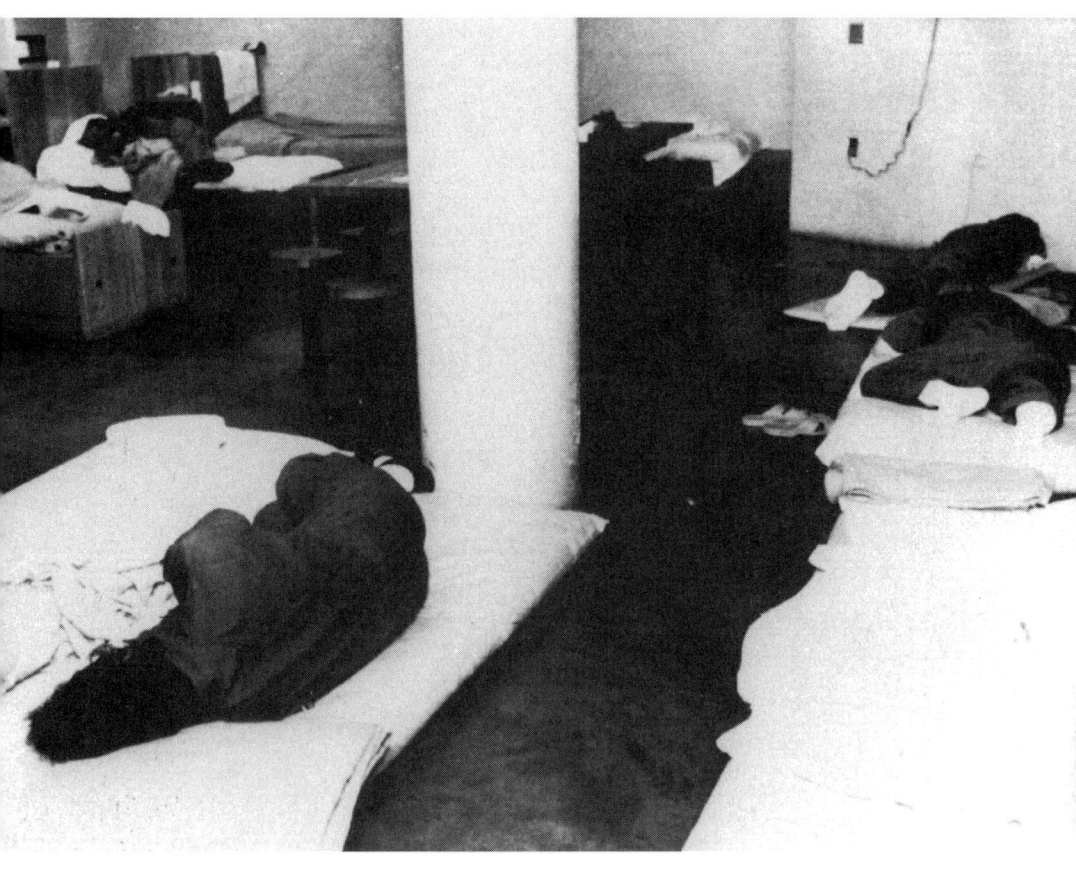

Due to the pressure of increased numbers, inmates at a county jail sleep on the floor.

jails, they *are* different. They house different types of inmates. Prisons hold people who have been convicted and are serving time for a serious crime, or a felony, which usually means a sentence of over a year. Jails house people held for traffic offenses; those serving sentences of up to a year for misdemeanors; those who cannot post bail; and those waiting to go to court. Jails also hold people who have been found guilty and are awaiting sentencing before being sent to serve time in a state or federal penitentiary. These various groups of people in jail totaled 424,000 in 1991,[3] in addition to those serving time in prison.

Whether people are serving time in a jail or in a prison may not seem significant to those of us who have never even visited a cell. But statistics are compiled separately for the two facilities.

We would like to believe that all those who have been convicted of crimes are either in prison or in jail, that they are serving time behind bars and away from the general public, and that these prisons and jails are keeping us safe from criminals. Unfortunately this is not true. Most convicted criminals in the correctional system are on probation or parole. In 1994 an estimated 3.2 percent of all U.S. adults were either on parole or on probation: 2.8 million on probation, and about 671,000 on parole. One in every 22 men and one in every 138 women were under the supervision of the correctional system on any given day. These figures show that a very large number of offenders serve all or part of their sentences under supervision in the community, not locked up behind bars. In 1990 three-quarters of the total estimated 4.3 million offenders convicted of a crime were living outside prison. Since 1980, the number of people on probation or parole has grown by 163 percent.[4]

Yet all of our correctional facilities are filled over capacity, and most are under court order to reduce their inmate population.

Perhaps the most discouraging aspect of the criminal justice problem is reflected in the recidivism rate of prisoners—or the return to prison for new offenses. Felons—serving terms of a year or longer—make up over half the probation population, and the statistics for recidivism are shocking. A 1986 special report compiled by the Bureau of Justice Statistics from a sample study of seventeen states reported that within three years of sentencing, nearly two out of three offenders had been arrested for a new felony or had been charged with violating their supervision requirements. In 1986 about 79,000 felons were placed on probation. Within three years, 43 percent were rearrested for a felony, and half of the arrests were for violent crimes such as murder, rape, robbery, or aggravated assault. Of the probationers followed, 62 percent had either violated a condition of their probation, such as testing positive for illegal drugs, or were rearrested for a new felony. About 84 percent had been ordered to pay a financial penalty, such as victim restitution, court costs, or probation supervision fees. Fewer than half of these had paid their penalty in full.[5] These statistics show that a large percentage of persons found guilty of a crime serious enough to serve time had been released into the community and either committed new crimes or did not comply with the court order for the original crime.

A close look at the American system of justice leads to a feeling of hopelessness. We spend billions of dollars on criminal justice—housing, feeding, and supervising criminals—but the rate of recidivism is at a record level. We are rearresting many of the same people over and over again.

But most important, we as a society must recognize the danger of having large numbers of people under conditional supervision, and we must question the ability of authorities to supervise and monitor the growing number of felons on probation—up from 2 million in 1985 to 3.2 million in 1994.

According to the U.S. Department of Justice, "probation" is defined as "a criminal sentence that requires the offender to meet conditions under supervision in the community." A probation officer usually monitors the offender and reports to the criminal justice system on whether or not the conditions of probation have been met.

The number of people sentenced directly to probation is alarming. In 1986, 31 percent of felons, instead of being sentenced to serve time, were placed on probation. They were required to have regular visits with a probation officer, but they were not confined to prison or jail. Another 21 percent received sentences that involved first confinement and then probation. Over 40 percent of those on probation were then convicted of a new felony. This rate of recidivism calls into question the idea of probation. As such a high percentage of offenders violate probation, committing new crimes when they have not even served their sentence for the original offense, probation becomes, in part, an issue of public safety.

The probation period is supposed to provide offenders with supervision to help them to a productive way of life. But the criminal justice system seems overwhelmed by the millions of offenders on probation living in communities. Many cannot remove themselves from the environment that led them into crime in the first place. Many end up back in confinement for their original crime after breaking probation, or behind bars to serve time for an additional crime against an additional set of victims.

To some people it seems clear that our system is simply not working. And unfortunately the public's fear and sense of hopelessness concerning crime is supported by the statistics. We have far too many prisoners behind bars, far too many criminals out in the community requiring supervision, and far too many who return to the community and commit new, serious crimes. The result seems to be that the public is at risk. So, while President Bush's use of the Willie Horton commercial to brand Governor Dukakis and the Democratic Party as soft on crime was a political ploy, the truth is that our system does not serve us well.

All people, declares the United States Constitution, must be assumed innocent until proven guilty. This concept is a basic tenet of American life. However, while we treasure this assurance of justice for all, it creates serious problems for the criminal justice system. All those who are arrested have the right to an attorney to represent them. Further, all those who have been charged with a crime have the right to a fair trial in court, or they may plead guilty to a lesser charge and be sentenced to serve for that lesser crime. Most crimes—89 percent, in fact—do not end up in a courtroom trial like those we see on television. The prosecuting and defending attorneys and the judge settle the case outside the courtroom. The number of cases has forced the courts to function far beyond their normal capacity, and defendants awaiting trial face long delays. In this situation, a court may allow plea bargaining, a common practice in the American legal system. The defendant offers to plead guilty to a lesser charge in return for a lesser penalty—a shorter prison term or a probation period. If the accused person seems likely to be found guilty, he or she is likely to plea-bargain.

In theory, plea bargaining is a way to speed up the court process. However, this procedure can lead to the future victimization of members of the community. With heavy court backlogs leading courts to accept plea bargaining, reduced sentences, and probation or parole, a majority of those convicted are now released into the community on probation or parole. Only 28 percent of convicted offenders were in confinement in 1993. However, the high recidivism rate of offenders indicates that a large percentage of criminals will be repeatedly arrested and will again plead guilty to a lesser charge and be released. As a result, a significant number of offenders are living among us, and some are committing serious crimes. As repeat offenders, or recidivists, they are likely to commit crimes that are more serious than their original crime.

To sum up, our criminal justice system encourages plea bargaining. Offenders are given lighter punishment by agreeing to plead guilty to a lesser crime. In return, we save taxpayers' money and the time of the courts by avoiding costly, time-consuming trials, which could still end with the offender going free.

Many people argue that we have an archaic system that worked earlier in our history, but is now detrimental to our society. Others argue just as forcefully that while we have a system that is cumbersome and costly, this country must protect the right of all citizens to a fair trial by a jury of their peers.

Chapter Three

The Young Offender

The incarceration of youngsters, with the possibility that their future lives might be spent going in and out of institutions, is a new and tragic development. Never in history have people been imprisoned at such early ages. Our overflowing jails and prisons now house a large population of young offenders who will grow up supervised by strangers, to whom they will be only numbers in cells.

These children will make their home behind bars and will never have the normal experiences of growing up with a family: playing in the park, coming home late from a date, staying after school, fighting with their brothers, and planning for happier futures.

A 1987 national survey by the Bureau of Justice Statistics showed that, of the 25,000 individuals confined to state-operated long-term juvenile institutions, an estimated 60.5 percent were between the ages of fifteen and seventeen; 12.4 percent were fourteen and younger; and 27.8 percent were eighteen or older. Thus, nearly three-quarters were under seventeen years of age. Almost half had been arrested

The correctional system is now housing an alarming number of young offenders.

more than three times, and over 20 percent had been arrested more than ten times. Furthermore, four out of five of these juveniles had been on probation previously, and three out of five had been committed to a correctional institution at least once before.[1] More than 90 percent were males; a disproportionate number (based on the country's total population) were black, 41.5 percent, and Latino, 18.9 percent; and 53 percent were white. Native Americans, Asians, and Pacific Islanders made up 5.7 percent.[2] The Bureau of Justice statistics survey also reported that over 60 percent of these youngsters were drug users; over 40 percent were under the influence of drugs when they were arrested, and over 40 percent were held for a violent offense.[3] So we are not talking about youngsters who run away from home or commit minor offenses like shoplifting a pencil.

For many of these youngsters, involvement with the criminal justice system has been a familiar pattern of life. More than half of all residents of state juvenile institutions reported that a family member had been incarcerated at some time. The profile of this group points to a life of failure and hopelessness.

An alarming number of America's children are in custody, and this will have a devastating effect on the rest of society. In 1994, more than 100,000 juveniles were held in custody. Further, about 20,000 of these youngsters were treated as adults, due to the seriousness of their crimes.[4]

Most of these youngsters are uneducated. While 76 percent of the general population of this age group has completed eight years of school, only 41 percent of the residents in these institutions had finished that level of schooling. Only 9.6 percent of them had completed high school.[5] Seven out of ten from this group grew up in a single-parent household, and over 50 percent had a family member incarcerated.⁶

These are the statistics that surveys and studies present. But what do they mean to the children in custody and to the general population? I talked to several kids, some still inside these institutions, others recently released and living in group homes, and some living in temporary homes without any permanency in their lives.

Bill expresses the hopelessness that seems pervasive among this group. He was one of three children born to an unmarried teenage mother. His father, an occasional drug user, came around sometimes. "It's better than some other kids have. At least I knew my father," he says with a shrug of his shoulders. His father and cousin were both incarcerated, and he spent his early childhood with his grandmother. His mother was young, without a job, trying to raise her children. Bill was born when she was sixteen, another child when she was seventeen, and the third when she was twenty. As a young single parent, his mother had to cope with three children. "All I remember is that she cried a lot. She was always frustrated, angry, and out of control. My father was in jail a lot, using drugs, getting arrested. He would come around and act sweet to her. Then he'd leave, and we wouldn't see him for months." Until Bill was five, he spent a lot of time with his grandmother and several cousins. But then his grandmother died and he moved back in with his mother, who was living with her friends, who were all on public assistance. He was a terrible student. He failed the third grade and probably had an undiagnosed learning disability. He was disruptive, got into fights, and had a very short attention span. He left school after the sixth grade and began to hang out on the street and use drugs. According to Bill, his mother didn't care, or she may have been overwhelmed. She began to drink more frequently and stay out, leaving her children with neighbors and friends.

Bill was first arrested for a crime at fourteen. He was shoplifting with friends—something that he considered "no big thing." "Everybody I know has done that," he says. By the time he was fifteen, he had been picked up dozens of times for transporting drugs, selling marijuana, picking pockets, shoplifting, stealing, and committing burglaries. Like 80 percent of juvenile offenders, he had already been on probation. Like 43 percent, he had been arrested more than five times—or perhaps, like 20 percent, it was ten times; he is not sure. Like over 50 percent of the youths in long-term institutions in 1987, his father was incarcerated, and like 60 percent of those in state-operated institutions, he was incarcerated for a crime that he had committed with others.[7] He stole cars in order to strip them and sell their parts, and with the rest of the group, he then spent his time and money getting high and hanging out. He stole to survive and to get high.

Bill is a young black male, uneducated, with numerous arrests on his record, who has been in and out of state institutions. Unlike some other youths who talk about big plans for the future and about getting out of the institution, Bill almost seems to believe that this is a normal life—the life that he and his friends are used to and expect. "You know, in my neighborhood, I never saw a black man who had anything go to work and come home," he says. "I saw these fat women go to work, come home late at night, afraid of being mugged or shot. They worked all day as maids or at some hospital, and still they couldn't pay the rent. I really did not see how that was so hip. I really don't think it makes any difference." He speaks without much expression, staring into space. To Bill and other youngsters, the institution is a place where they have friends. They miss the streets, the excitement, and the drugs, though several claim they use drugs even inside the facility. They wait to go back to the streets without any plans about where they'll go or what will happen.

Calling Bill and his friends "youngsters" doesn't ring true. They are not children. They are profoundly ignorant in many areas, yet they know a lot about things that most adults never care to know about and would never want to experience. They all claim to have gone to bed hungry at some point in their few years. They have all learned about sex from personal experience, although their youth shows in their giggles and smirks as they proudly say yes, they "know how to make babies." Perhaps sex is the only aspect of their lives where they feel they have some control. The only white adults they knew were teachers and a few social workers and probation officers, many of whom believed that the boys were stupid and inferior. They had talked to some white store owners and had seen white cops patrol their neighborhood. Many claimed to have owned a gun, though they would not admit to having used it—lately.

To people outside this hopeless cycle, it seems that these young people should be willing to do anything to change their lives, since they must see that crime will lead to repeated incarcerations and the road to nowhere. But I found that while they all claimed they would never return to an institution, jails don't scare them. They are not places that are foreign to them. In jail they can meet new friends and learn to commit new crimes. They can dare each other to commit crimes that are bold and suggest toughness, and they can dream of schemes that will make them rich. They watch a lot of television, and if they can, they blast rap music, get into fights, and are absorbed by "Lifestyles of the Rich and Famous"—a picture of the life they want. Few of the youngsters seem interested in finishing high school, and some are embarrassed by their inability to learn. Instead of learning, they rebel. They act hostile and give their teachers a difficult time. Among this group, being a good student is not a badge of honor; being "bad" is the right and manly thing to be. They laugh at any display of love, and they feel sorry for no one, certainly not for the people they hurt while committing a crime. They often say that they had no intention of hurting anyone, but if someone was in the wrong place at the wrong time, they feel little remorse for hurting them.

Juvenile offenders are a challenge to the correctional system. What should we do with youngsters who commit serious crimes? If we incarcerate them for three to five years (the minimum sentence most felons now serve), they may become hardened criminals. But serious crimes warrant this punishment, and society demands that those who commit them be treated as adults.

Some social scientists suggest that the legal economy offers these youngsters few opportunities. Selling drugs has thus become an occupation for thousands of uneducated, unskilled, unemployed teenagers. The hope of making quick money selling drugs on the streets leads these kids to run the high risk of being arrested. Facing fewer options and greater obstacles, African-American and Latino youths are more likely than white youths to sell drugs. They often start in their own neighborhood by supplying drugs to their friends. Once they begin dealing, their easy access to drugs makes them vulnerable to becoming users themselves and becoming addicted to the drugs they distribute.

Living in neighborhoods overrun by drug dealers and other criminals, and finding few opportunities, many teenagers are drawn to crime as a way to escape.

The next step in this tragic progression is usually a drug arrest. Once arrested, they are even less likely to be able to find legitimate work. As African-Americans or Latinos, they face prejudice; they are poor, uneducated, unskilled, and now they have an arrest record. In order to survive, many continue to commit crimes, selling and perhaps using drugs. But when they reach eighteen, the law changes. For the same offense, they will now probably receive a mandatory sentence of 6.5 years. Upon release, nearly 75 percent will return to the same activities and be rearrested. Many of these repeat offenders will make their homes behind bars for the rest of their lives.[8]

Lack of, or inadequate, education is often a nearly insurmountable obstacle to finding a way out of the poverty-crime-prison cycle. The children most at risk of failing educationally are from single-parent households, live in poverty, have parents with little education, have siblings who have dropped out of school, and are often home with no adult supervision. In the black community, 46 percent of families were led by a single parent in 1988. Among white families, that figure is 17.7 percent. Nearly half, or 47 percent, of black wage earners are paid less than $15,000. Only 14 percent of whites and 37.5 percent of Hispanics earned less than $15,000. Black and Hispanic eighth-graders spent more time unsupervised; nearly 20 percent spent three hours a day alone while 12 percent of white eighth-graders and 16.3 percent of Latino children were alone at that age. In all five risk areas listed above (single parent, parents without high school diploma, low income, sibling dropped out of school, home alone for extended periods), black youngsters suffered the most. Hispanic children were also at greater risk than whites.[9]

In 1989, among black thirteen-year-olds who had reached eighth grade, 51.5 percent of males and 38 percent of females were below grade level, according to the National Center for Education Statistics. Poor school performance, being left back with younger children, and being embarrassed and frustrated in crowded classrooms can lead to dropping out of school. Black dropouts with few skills are more likely to be unemployed and unemployable. Unable to be wage earners, or as low wage earners, they may be attracted by the lure of quick cash through drugs, and once that happens they are on their way to getting arrested and serving time. According to a U.S. Department of Justice report, between 1985 and 1986 the number of juveniles sentenced to detention centers as a result of drug charges increased by 21 percent. In the same period, the number of nonwhite juveniles referred to reformatories by juvenile courts increased by 42 percent. This increase in referrals, coupled with stiffer punishments for drug offenders, resulted in a 71 percent rise in the number of nonwhite youths detained for drug-related offenses.[10]

Although the National Drug Control Policy was directed toward reducing the drug supply, the supply does not seem to have been significantly affected. Instead, the criminal justice system has been overloaded with low-level drug offenders. In periodic drug sweeps, we arrest and rearrest low-level street distributors in low-income areas. A large number of black and minority youths live in these areas, which places them in the likely position of being arrested. In addition, the nation's mandatory sentence for drug offenses has tripled, from 2.2 years in 1985 to 6.5 years in 1992[11] and has led, in part, to major prison overcrowding.

These problems affect all of us. Juvenile facilities are vastly overcrowded. Each institutionalized youth costs taxpayers and society $40,000 to $100,000 a year. Juvenile detention centers have become warehouses for young people. Society has dumped these youngsters on the correctional system.

Some are homeless, some are emotionally disturbed, and many are well below their grade level in education but too proud to admit it. Yet they won't acknowledge any reason to get an education. We tell children to say no to drugs, but many of these youngsters have known drugs all their lives and are too defiant to listen to anything an adult tells them. Many are already hardened and hostile, concealing warmth out of fear of being labeled a "faggot" or a "wimp." Carrying a gun establishes that they have "class" and earns them respect. Those working with youthful inmates observe that, sadly, most of them will go through the system many times. No one can persuade them to leave their way of life behind until they are able to see something better.

Many young offenders told me chilling stories of seeing their friends die, some accidentally caught by gunfire, others trying to settle a score or a drug-related "beef." They do not expect to live a long time—maybe twenty-five years. Unfortunately, in the black community, statistics suggest that their expectations about life are based on reality.

The crisis in the black community is so alarming that federal officials are addressing it not as a criminal problem but as a health problem. At the Centers for Disease Control and Prevention in Atlanta, a department is dedicated to reducing violence—the number one cause of death among black men age fifteen to twenty-four. Between 1985 and 1989 homicides increased 74 percent among young black males, according to the secretary of Health and Human Services. Now young black males are almost fourteen times as likely to be homicide victims as are other people, with 114 homicides per 100,000. And, alarmingly, two-thirds were committed by persons under age twenty-one.[12]

Today we can conquer many illnesses. Life expectancy of the overall population is 75.3 years. Yet young people are dying—not of illness, but of homicide. Many of these young people are too young to enter military service or to vote, and they are certainly too young to die. With no other hopes or goals, many young offenders aspire to be big-time drug dealers with expensive cars, and to be the most feared members of a gang.

Many young offenders commit extremely serious crimes, some of which are heinous. These teenagers often seem fearless, perhaps because of peer pressure or because of the heavy use of crack, a drug that is especially violence-provoking. Thirty-three convicted murderers who committed their crimes before the age of eighteen are now on death row, waiting to be executed. Of the thirty-six states that have death penalty laws, twenty-two have established a minimum age for execution (twelve is the youngest age). In 1988, the U.S. Supreme Court ruled that a fifteen-year-old in Oklahoma could not be executed. Thus sixteen is the minimum age at which a person can be executed if a state does not have its own law setting a minimum age.[13] These children are not old enough to get an abortion without parental consent in most states, or even buy a pack of cigarettes, yet can be sentenced to death.

What do we do with these possibly dangerous criminals who have been found guilty of horrible crimes? Keep them in prison for life at an enormous cost? Execute them? Release them to endanger others and become part of the record number of males between fifteen and twenty-four who will be killed on the streets of the world's largest democracy, the nation with the most schools and one of the highest standards of living?

Chapter Four

Women in Prison

Institutions for females are different from those that house males. Bridget Gladwin, superintendent of the Taconic Correctional Facility for Women, a medium security institution in Bedford Hills, New York, a quiet suburban community, sums it up: "All you have to see is the difference in the visiting room." At men's prisons, women come to visit, bringing food, clothes, gifts, and even money. Ironically, even men who had no girlfriends before they were incarcerated seem to find one to visit them in prison. Women prisoners, however, are visited by their families—their mothers, sisters, and children—and a few friends. They are rarely visited by brothers, boyfriends, husbands, or the fathers of their children.

Women in prison still constitute a small percentage of the total prison population in the United States. But as with juveniles, there has been a radical

Taconic Correctional Facility in New York State.

change in the ten years from 1980 to 1990. The number of women under jurisdiction of state and federal prisons increased 200 percent, setting a new record. However, even after this enormous increase, females still accounted for only 5.7 percent of prisoners at the end of 1989.[1]

According to the Bureau of Justice Statistics Special Report, "Women in Prison," for every 100,000 men in the resident population, 549 were serving a prison sentence of more than one year, compared to 31 women for the same population. This is a significant difference, and it has contributed to the changes that have occurred for incarcerated women in these ten years. Each year more and more women are incarcerated for drug-related crimes. More of them are H.I.V. positive, meaning that they carry the virus that causes AIDS, and about 78 percent are mothers, most of children under eighteen years of age. In the last ten years, we have also seen an increase in female drug offenders serving time. About 40 percent were using drugs daily, and at least a third were on drugs at the time of their arrest.

About 60 percent of the women have been convicted of nonviolent crimes, such as fraud, larceny, and theft. The remaining 40 percent of women prisoners have been sentenced for a violent crime; nearly half of those for homicide. Surprisingly, the women were more likely than men to have victimized a male. (Violent men victimized women in 52.7 percent of the cases.) Many of the women prisoners—61 percent—reported that they had had a close relationship with their victim. In over one-third of these cases, the male victim was a relative or intimate—that is, a boyfriend or husband. Male inmates were more likely than females to victimize strangers.

A second important statistic points to a difference between men and women serving time for homicide. Women were sentenced for the homicide of a relative or an intimate in 25 percent of the cases as opposed to 6 percent for men. A third, and compelling, figure revealed in the "Women in Prison" study is that 41 percent of incarcerated women reported that they had endured sexual or physical abuse. By 1991, that figure had risen to 50 percent. The women incarcerated for a violent offense were the most likely to have been abused, both sexually and physically. Many of the women who committed a violent crime shot or maimed the man who was abusing them.

Women, like men, have a very high rate of recidivism. Two-thirds of the women in prison were previously sentenced to probation or were incarcerated as juveniles or adults. Almost half were sentenced to incarceration or probation at least twice before. Over 10 percent have been through the system more than six times. So, like men, these women are caught in the cycle of committing a crime, getting arrested, serving time, being released, and committing another crime. Fewer than half the women in prison had jobs when they were arrested, but more women than men had finished high school or attended college. The contrasting profile of male prisoners reveals that they were twice as likely as female offenders to have a prior conviction. An estimated 31 percent of women serving time in state prisons had no prior sentence of any nature. Fewer women than men had six or more prior convictions. Only 8 percent of women prisoners, as opposed to 21 percent of male prisoners serving time for a violent crime, had been previously convicted of a violent offense.

In summary, women are more likely to commit

nonviolent offenses. When they do commit a violent crime it is often the homicide of a relative or intimate who has abused them. Women commit far fewer violent crimes than men, and are less likely to victimize strangers. The number of drug-related offenses and cases of drug abuse increased dramatically for both sexes between 1980 and 1990. Arrests for possession and sale of drugs increased by 307 percent for women; for men there was a 147 percent increase in drug-related arrests.

Walking into a female prison feels very different from entering a male institution. At a male prison perhaps the sheer number of inmates and the violent nature of the men—many serving life sentences—create a tension that surrounds you as soon as you walk through the gates. Taconic Correctional Facility for Women—which was a male facility in the 1980s—is an example of how the correctional system has adapted to the increase in the female inmate population. The facility looks like a summer camp, except for the barbed wire and fence around it. Bridget Gladwin, the superintendent (the title now used instead of "warden"), doesn't look like the prison officials you've seen in movies. She's small, gentle-looking, has a warm smile, and seems very caring. Her training is in drug treatment programs. She works in a separate house on the prison grounds, with no bars, fences, or electronic devices. When I met her, she had just moved her office and was digging through packed boxes while a male inmate on loan from Sing Sing, a men's facility in Ossining, New York, was hanging pictures on the walls. We talked about prisons while her phones rang nonstop. A twenty-year veteran of the correctional system, she now presides over a facility that is using progressive methods to respond to a growing prison population of women with a wide range of problems, including many who have been incarcerated for drug or alcohol-related crimes, and a huge number—nearly 80 percent—who are mothers and are responsible for the lives of their children.

The drug offenders at the Taconic Correctional Facility are in a federally funded program called CASAT (Comprehensive Alcohol, Substance Abuse Treatment). The inmates participate in a six-month program that involves stages of counseling and group therapy to help them deal with their substance-abuse problems. The program also provides education and vocational training. After completing CASAT, the inmates are paroled into a early-release program.

Taconic has over four hundred women. Three hundred take part in the drug-and alcohol-abuse program that occupies most of their time. Twenty-three women in this unit have babies who live with them. At Taconic, this special program for women and their infants is housed in a separate area called the nursery. The nursery looks like a recreation room in any residence hall, with a colorful happy birthday banner hung on the wall, a television set, a couch, and a few worn chairs. Pam, who directs the parenting program, showed me around with great pride and commented, "We just celebrated two children's birthdays." Under this program, inmates who give birth while serving a sentence can keep their babies with them, in their own rooms, for a year. If the mother has to serve more time after that, however, the child must leave the prison. The women's rooms do not follow prison standards. They look like rooms in a college dormitory. There are no window bars or exposed toilets of the sort seen in some prisons. Two women share each of the small rooms, which are often crowded with decorations, cribs, baby paraphernalia, and diapers.

Considering the circumstances, the babies look surprisingly healthy. None of them cried during my visit. They all seemed to be outgoing infants, well developed and active. Some were trying to stand up or crawl, and they smiled at every newcomer. Their mothers fussed over them as they discussed whether the children should be given cereal along with their bottles. Some said it helped the babies sleep through the night while others argued that it might be good for the mothers if their babies slept through, but it was not good for the babies. The CASAT program includes daily parenting and hygiene classes along with counseling, therapy, and other aspects of drug-abuse treatment. The mothers' schedules include taking the babies outside the building to the park or to their backyard. When they are at their substance-abuse meetings, other women baby-sit for them for a few dollars a week.

The lives of these women seem hectic. They have to get up very early, feed their babies, and be showered and dressed by eight, ready for their chores or for a program session or parenting class. In this facility, watching television is not allowed during the day. The women buzz around, carrying the babies down several flights of stairs, taking them outside in strollers, and attending group counseling for substance abuse in the yard.

When this comprehensive program for parenting was introduced, many people, including the superintendent, had reservations about it. The idea that prisons should house babies with their mothers seemed daring and is still not universally accepted by correctional professionals. However, after seeing this facility it seems to me that no one could doubt that these babies are better off than they would be on the outside. The women, many of whom were mothers for the first time (at least in the sociological sense if not also

At the Taconic Correctional Facility and at some other women's prisons, mothers can have their babies live with them for a time.

in the biological sense), are living in a healthier environment than they knew in the outside world, with its terrible pressures of drugs, poverty, family problems, and abuse. While incarcerated, these women share a room with another woman in the same situation, watch out for each other's babies, take turns caring for them, and spend almost all their waking hours bonding with their babies.

These women look like caring mothers, not like criminals. Some are healthier and stronger than they ever were and have gained 20 or 30 pounds since incarceration. For some, this is the first time they have eaten three meals a day, stayed off drugs, not worked as prostitutes, received medical attention, and lived structured lives.

Considering the frightening recidivism rate of over 75 percent for women and over 80 percent for men, it is encouraging to see a program that appears to be a comprehensive model for helping mothers and their babies. Pam, the program's director, is convinced that most of the women "make it" on the outside after they complete the prison program. "All these women leave here and say they will never touch drugs again," she says. While we know that, unfortunately, this is not true, many of them stay in touch with Pam, and her bulletin board is filled with pictures of smiling, healthy-looking children. Pam adds, "If a year of bonding with a baby twenty-four hours a day doesn't keep you off drugs, then I don't know what will."

Many of the women follow their term at Taconic with a stay a Providence House, a halfway house in

A residential facility in Pennsylvania houses women offenders and their children.

Brooklyn, New York, which takes women who have been released from prison, along with their children. At Providence House, the parenting and child-care instruction emphasized in the nursery program at Taconic is continued, and the residence serves as a stepping-stone for women who are afraid to go back to their families or their old neighborhoods and who need additional support to put their lives together. Pam and the rest of the Taconic staff know of only one woman who failed after completing both programs.

The institution has little control over what happens to the babies after they leave. If a mother hasn't completed her sentence by the time the baby is a year old and must be taken away, the mother's cries can be heard throughout the facility, according to a guard. In most cases, a maternal grandmother or relative takes the baby, often bringing it back to visit, along with older children, if they have not been placed in foster care or in child-care institutions.

Are we too soft on these convicts, some critics ask. One mother explained her feelings: "As someone who gave birth and then returned to prison never having seen my baby, I can tell you that being with her this time made all the difference in the world." This mother, a former drug user now in the Taconic nursery program, admitted she had not been a good mother to her first child. She knew nothing about being a parent, and spent all her time chasing drugs and getting high. Now, after a fourth arrest and third conviction, she had given birth while incarcerated. She is in the substance-abuse treatment program, lives with her baby, and feels that the baby will keep her from going back to jail. Her boyfriend, who had also served time but was released from prison, never came to visit her or his child.

"Most of these women have no business being inside a prison," commented one staff member, a long-time veteran of the system. As many prison officials point out, women prisoners are different from men prisoners. Many of these women began to use drugs as teenagers, through their boyfriends or because of peer pressure. Their drug habit led them into crime, and many have been left with children fathered by the same men who got them involved in drugs and then into prostitution to support their drug habits. Yet once the women are incarcerated, these men will have nothing to do with them.

In addition, their use of intravenous drugs places many of these women at high risk of H.I.V. infection. Many don't get tested for H.I.V. because they do not want to know if they're infected, and testing is not mandatory for prisoners in New York State. Some worry that their babies may carry the virus. Although the ones I saw looked healthy, H.I.V. tests on babies are not accurate until the children are about fifteen months old.

This drug-treatment program, like many programs developed in the 1960s, is based on discipline and structure, and includes vocational and educational training. The Taconic facility, however—unlike some male institutions, where inmates are taught carpentry, auto repair, or mechanical skills—offers only a few vocational training opportunities. The participants are screened, and all correctional professionals agree that if an inmate is not ready to be rehabilitated, the prison staff can do nothing but wait until she returns for another term.

Those attending drug treatment programs are busy all afternoon. In group settings, they talk with counselors and members of their therapy group. They are supervised by a tough but caring counselor known by all the inmates and trusted by many of them. Two inmates work with the counselor and are trusted to enter data into the prison computers that could affect an inmate's life, causing her to be admitted to or eliminated from the treatment program or assigned to another group level. One inmate asked to be readmitted to the program. "No," the counselor decided. "She was already in the program, then she wanted out, then she came back. She's not ready." "How about Hernandez?" asked a cheerful Hispanic woman who has been the counselor's assistant for over a year. "Yes, Hernandez can move to the next level of the program." Another inmate wanted a new roommate. The counselor denied the request without any discussion: "No, you have to learn to get along with people." Turning to me he explained, "These people need to learn discipline on every level. If we moved everybody who wanted to be moved that's what we'd be doing all day—moving people."

Superintendent Gladwin made a point that other correctional officials echoed. The prison system cannot rehabilitate inmates because most of them were never "habilitated"—that is, socialized, or prepared to live in society. They have never had any structure in their lives—in school, at home, or anyplace else. The prison system is expected to rehabilitate people the rest of society has rejected: people they don't know what to do with, people who are uneducated, undisciplined, and untrained. Some could not tell time or read before they came to prison. Some had emotional problems. Some had been severely abused. And 41 percent of females in prison—at Taconic and elsewhere—have abused drugs and alcohol. So the correctional system, in addition to providing punishment, is expected to send individuals back to society (after just two to three years in most cases) with job skills and with the ability to get to work on time, stay off drugs and alcohol, find a new neighborhood, make new friends, and sometimes reject the family that helped contribute to a life on the streets.

In New York State, prisoners can be eligible for an early-release program two years before the end of their sentence. In early release, they can go to work in the community during the daytime and return to prison for the night. Work-release programs provide transition, enabling some people to make it into another lifestyle and become law-abiding citizens. "We are testing people," said the superintendent. "We are giving them an opportunity to take part in treatment and to go out into the early-release program and see if they can get a job." But many who are not ready or who are unable to change will just keep returning until they decide that they will do anything to stay out of prison.

"The legislators have to decide how they want to spend the taxpayers' money. Drug treatment is costly, so they decide to spend the money on building prisons instead. We already have sixty prisons in New York State alone. How many more prisons can we build?" She added, "However, now there is much greater leeway to develop alternatives to incarceration. Inmates can go into drug treatment, go into treatment outside of prison, or enter a work-release program. Over a billion dollars in tax revenue goes into prisons in this state. How much more money can you put into this thing?"

All those who work with female prisoners agree that while the women's institutions seem less severe, the road back to life in society is harder for them. The majority of the women used drugs and worked as prostitutes to support their habit. A woman with a history of addiction and prostitution, and with chil-

In the common area at a women's prison, inmates gather to watch television.

dren to care for, will have difficulty finding a job. In addition, these women have very low self-esteem. Some are in psychological pain and have been badly damaged. Furthermore, many halfway houses and work-release programs are not equipped to house their children, which makes it almost impossible for the mothers to start a new life. Therefore, when the women leave the facilities, they often fall once again under the influence of some man who is able to undo all the progress and work of rehabilitation. The inmates and the staff agree that no one can help these women until they are ready to take the difficult road away from the streets, away from old friends and destructive families, and away from the only life they have known for many years—a life of crime.

In prison almost all of the women seem ready to make the change. They are all resolved never to go back. But the real test comes once they reenter society. In prison they are protected, they have company, they are away from the people and circumstances that led them into drugs, alcohol, and crimes. Many, for the first time in years, are able to think clearly, without the influence of drugs.

Visitors who see inmates in prison, off drugs, may not be aware of the danger. As the women cuddle their babies, it is easy to forget that many are violent offenders who, not long ago, left their children at home alone or with a neighbor, and then went out to steal, to sell their bodies, and to shoot drugs, not thinking about the consequences.

When I was researching my first book on prisons, I found the women very chatty; they wanted to tell me their stories. This has not changed over the years.

Lydia is a trusted inmate who works with sensitive information for the prison staff. She looks like any clerical worker on the outside. When we spoke, she was in pretty good spirits, considering her history. She and her boyfriend had been arrested for committing a burglary to steal money for drugs. Lydia's boyfriend testified against her and was given a reduced sentence. Like many women with similar stories, she had used drugs "casually" for two years with friends and then had become addicted, using daily any drug she could get her hands on. Like many other offenders, she had previous arrests for which she had received probation. But this time she was sentenced to eight years in prison for a burglary committed without a weapon (more than the maximum mandatory sentence for armed robbery). During her incarceration, she finished her drug-abuse treatment program, completed two years of college, and mapped out a future education program that includes plans to earn a master's degree. She has two more years to serve before she will be eligible for parole, but she has a supportive family and seems ready to leave prison and never return.

While Lydia was telling her story, Carolyn, another inmate, was bragging about the white-collar crime she had committed—embezzling checks. She admitted writing over a quarter of a million dollars in checks, taking other people's life insurance money. Carolyn and other convicts like her minimize and justify their crimes by saying, "I did not hurt anyone, at least not physically." She told her story with ease, although the officials said that she embellished some of the details. She had on several occasions been arrested for elaborate schemes in which bank tellers cashed forged checks for her in return for kickbacks. I wondered how she was able to come up with these schemes. "I used to work at the bank as a teller." She smiled as she gave the explanation. She made it seem easy, and I understood why a large percentage of female offenders commit this type of crime. White-collar fraud can be especially tempting to women in low-paying clerical jobs who are trying to support several children and who process millions of dollars through credit-card and computer transactions.

"What prompted you to start this scheme?" I asked Carolyn. "It was easy," she said. After the first few forged checks she grew bolder and more daring, took more money, and was caught. She claimed that she had children to support, but actually she used the money to buy cars, clothing, and flashy jewelry. While she seemed smart, as she had demonstrated devising elaborate schemes, I wondered if prison would really change her. A counseling program known as Money Addiction is offered for inmates like her, but she laughed at the thought of attending. She is angry because the staff won't let her work in the prison office near the computers. The superintendent comments, "When people are in danger of losing their house, or can't feed their children on twenty thousand dollars a year, and think they have found a way to steal hundreds of thousands of dollars seemingly without risk, how can you persuade them to stop? These are the people hardest to change."

The prison bars closed behind me as I walked out into a beautiful sunny day in the country. I left the prison grounds and recalled one staff member's comments: "Being in here, pregnant or caring for a baby in prison alone, and losing your freedom must be the most horrifying experience that anyone can imagine." For some it may take many cycles of crime-incarceration-release before they are ready to live in society, never to return to prison. This program might just be a catalyst for that change.

Chapter Five

AIDS: The New Challenge

The correctional system is a microcosm of society, and so must deal with all the ills and problems of the society. Drug abuse, AIDS, and tuberculosis (TB) are among the problems the prison system faces.

In 1980, AIDS was not a household word and, to our knowledge, no one had died of the disease. Crack was not a part of our vocabulary, and the common belief was that cocaine, the drug of choice for some wealthy people, was not addictive. The number of heroin addicts, estimated at about 1.5 million in 1971, was reported to have decreased significantly.[1] Against this backdrop, there was reason to hope that the prison population would decline, and that the country—led by a new Republican administration promising to be tough on crime—would make some progress in reducing crime.

But that promise died as the 1980s progressed. The deadly and fear-inspiring illness, AIDS, appeared. White-collar crime became rampant, and well-known Wall Street figures were caught illegally trading hundreds of millions of dollars. Crack—a dangerous, highly addictive, and violence-provoking drug—

swept through the inner cities. In response, we built a record number of prisons to house many of those propelled into crime by an addiction to crack, along with a few well-dressed millionaires like Ivan Boesky, who were sent to federal prisons for making money illegally on the stock market.

We as a society began to learn about AIDS and H.I.V., the virus that causes the illness. But as we focused on transmission of the virus through sexual activity, particularly in the homosexual community, H.I.V. infection spread rapidly among intravenous drug users. Addicts who shared needles for drug use became the group with the fastest-growing number of cases of AIDS. The overtaxed prison system was not prepared to cope with a challenge as overwhelming as AIDS. We are still learning about the deadly virus, and research continues. New drugs are being developed, and there are some that may prolong the lives of patients infected by the virus who have not yet developed full-blown AIDS.

Through the decade the correctional system was stretched to its limit—by massive overcrowding, a significant increase in violent inmates, inmates with drug- and alcohol-abuse problems, and by severe budget cuts that forced staff reductions. In addition, the Sentencing Reform Act, which took effect in November 1987, established guidelines for mandatory sentences and called for judges to increase prison time in proportion to the seriousness of an offense. Thus, the number of prisoners increased substantially.

In most prisons large groups of inmates function in unison. Hundreds of prisoners eat together, get up and go to bed at the same time, and live in a very structured, tightly controlled system. It is a world of serious offenders locked up in an overcrowded space, with daily outbursts of violence and problems of discipline. This overtaxed prison system was pushed even further when it faced the additional responsibility of responding to the AIDS crisis—even though we as a society still cannot cope with H.I.V.-infected people who are not in prison.

"Two systems have become the caretakers for all of society's ills—the school system and the prison system," says a prison superintendent who has served in the correctional system for over twenty years. "Society has dumped so many other problems on us that we are hardly in the business that we are supposed to be in—that is, the corrections business." He went on to say that we as a society aren't handling the flood of teenagers who are released from schools even though they can't read. A counselor added, "One of the inmates signed his name with an X. He couldn't even sign his name. I wonder how they let him out of the fourth grade." Another prison official said, "Teenage unemployment is an epidemic, yet the president is sending billions of dollars and planes, boats, and soldiers to fight drugs in South America—a tactic that has obviously not cut down on drugs in this country. So we take all those people that society does not want, and we put them in prison—the drug users, the uneducated and unemployed, those with AIDS." He added, "And then the government cuts our funds for staff and for treatment programs."

According to the Centers for Disease Control and Prevention (CDC), the total number of AIDS cases among inmates in U.S. federal, state and larger city correctional systems was 6,985 as of November 1990. In that year, 28 percent of all deaths in state prisons were AIDS related.[2] It should be noted that these estimates are considered very low by all officials. According to the CDC, prisons have the highest percentage of H.I.V. infection of any public institutions.

In October 1990 there were 17 cases of AIDS in the United States per 100,000 population, up from 14 in 1989. In state and federal prison systems, the figure ranged from 0 to 1,047 cases per 100,000. Twelve systems had rates of over 100 cases per 100,000.[3] The CDC reports that 4 percent of the nation's 4.3 million offenders tested in 1991 were carrying the virus. Canada reported 71 inmates with AIDS for the same period. In contrast, less than one-half of one percent in the general blood donor population tested positive.

A significant number of intravenous drug users support their habit through illegal activities. Thus they may be arrested and convicted of a crime, and are incarcerated. An increasing number carry H.I.V. infection. Many of these infected inmates are black or Hispanic, and a high percentage are females, due to the high level of I.V. drug use among women offenders.

The correctional system has been trying to find ways to manage this population. The issue of where H.I.V.-infected inmates belong is difficult. Initially, infected inmates in a number of institutions were isolated from the general population. Some preferred to be isolated. AIDS patients are very susceptible to disease, as their immune systems have been destroyed by H.I.V., and so they are concerned about living with the general population. They would be exposed to colds or other minor diseases that a healthy individual can easily fight, but that can be fatal to someone with AIDS. However, if an institution isolates these inmates, it may be liable for a court challenge and charged with discrimination against a specific group.

Healthy inmates have other concerns. They are afraid for their own health, and at times are cruel to the afflicted inmates. Since fights are daily occur-

rences in prison, they fear that if they are cut or scratched, they could be exposed to H.I.V. Non-infected inmates are also angry about sharing facilities, arguing that people with AIDS are often ill and might disrupt their sleep.

I met several men inside prison facilities who talked openly about AIDS, yet no one agreed about anything but the deep tragedy surrounding it. Those who share rooms with AIDS patients are afraid of being infected and feel that their rights have been violated. Yet, according to law, people with AIDS cannot be isolated and are entitled to confidentiality about their illness. Again the interests of the different people involved in this problem are in conflict. Infected inmates may be critically ill, requiring extensive medical attention, daily administration of prescribed drugs, and ongoing care. The prison system cannot provide all this without failing in some of its responsibilities to other inmates.

Whose rights are more important—those of the general inmate population or those of prisoners dying of this illness? This is a question that the correctional system is simply unable to answer, particularly at a time when it is desperately short of funds. Yet in New York State alone, more than $6 million was spent for drugs like AZT to help people with H.I.V. live longer before succumbing to full-blown AIDS.

Even those working with AIDS patients are sometimes at odds with one another. Those responsible for their medical care feel that the patients with AIDS are not receiving the type of medical attention they need. Some corrections officers feel that people who

In the close quarters of men's prisons, infectious diseases are easily spread.

commit crimes are in prison for punishment, and they consider inmates with AIDS an added aggravation. They view them as criminals, and they wonder why our tax dollars should be used to prolong their lives. They also point out that prisons are not set up for the care of special cases. A prison is meant to be a place of punishment and rehabilitation of individuals who have committed crimes. Privately, some corrections officers admit that they fear these inmates who have so little to lose. They feel the infected inmates can be dangerous, and they worry about the possibility that an inmate might purposely attempt to infect them with H.I.V.

If being incarcerated seems like a terrible life, being critically ill or dying in prison seems like the ultimate punishment. Some prison officials, including some very conservative administrators, suggest that once inmates are diagnosed with this illness, they should be released, as they cannot be treated properly inside a prison. Prison hospitals are not equipped to treat people who need a great deal of care and nursing.

Some prison officials and other observers feel that by keeping infected inmates in prison, we are slowly killing them, as they may not receive medical treatments that might be available outside an institution. In New York and some other states, legislation has been proposed for a medical parole bill. This bill would apply only to those inmates who are terminally ill, and the majority of those eligible would be AIDS patients. It is estimated that New York State could save $1.3 million each year by releasing fifty inmates with AIDS.

In New York City, it is estimated that one of every four people in jail is infected with H.I.V, and one of every five has tested positive for TB, according to the Department of Corrections. This means that the

Department of Corrections in New York City, already responsible for housing about 22,000 inmates daily (more than 17,000 who are awaiting trial or sentencing, and over 4,000 who have already been sentenced), manages a vast number of prisoners in need of ongoing intensive care in the prison hospital ward. The already overtaxed and understaffed system has to find ways to treat and manage these critically ill patients in an environment that offers no privacy, where inmates are only a few feet away from one another even during their sleeping hours. The system now also has the enormous task of trying to prevent the spread of H.I.V. through sexual contact and intravenous drug use. An additional problem is the alarming appearance of drug-resistant tuberculosis in prisons. TB is transmitted through the air, and AIDS patients, with damaged immune systems, are particularly susceptible.

The idea of releasing prisoners with AIDS is problematic. If we release AIDS patients, although they have been convicted of a crime, do we also release inmates who are dying of cancer or other illnesses? Some do not want to be released because—as horrible as it is to die behind bars—they know that while they're in prison they will get some medical care, be fed, and have a place to sleep. On the outside, these basic survival needs may not be filled. We know that a majority of the inmates who are H.I.V. positive are black or Hispanic, and a large percent are women.[4] Most of the women are intravenous drug users under thirty years of age. As seriously ill ex-convicts, they are unlikely to be able to support themselves outside prison. The cost of the AZT treatments alone would be too high for someone released from prison to manage. To pay for them, the released prisoners might resort to crime. It is discouraging to think that someone is better off staying in prison, and it's hard to imagine that anyone would prefer to stay inside, but outside the prison walls there is none of the care needed by individuals too ill to fend for themselves.

AIDS is a controversial issue in the correctional system. Debates focus on laws to protect the rights of patients and of the other inmates, the development of new drugs to keep patients alive longer, and questions about the state's responsibility to prolong convicts' lives. The law now mandates that patients are to receive AZT, a drug that helps some live longer. As new drugs are developed, the question of whether prison inmates should be given the treatment will be reviewed by the officials and doctors. The issue remains unresolved. Are we as a society obliged to help criminals live longer by keeping them on very expensive drugs? Or would we better serve the prison population and society as a whole if we instead invested some of our slim resources in projects that would help prisoners learn skills they could use once they leave prison?

There is no consensus even among inmates themselves about the best way to handle prisoners who are drug users and who can continue to spread H.I.V. inside the facilities. Some medical officials have urged that condoms and clean needles be given out to prison inmates to help prevent the spread of AIDS. Yet guards and prison officials say that providing condoms and needles would be a tacit admission that sexual activity and drug use are going on inside their facilities in blatant disregard of prison rules. Within this controversy we can see the sad irony: while we know that condoms and clean needles would slow the spread of this disease, clearly it would be difficult for prison officials to admit that they cannot control the inmates, and appear to condone drug use and sex among prisoners while society pays the bills with tax dollars.

Some officials argue that instead of paying for expensive drugs for inmates, the government should invest in better medical care for senior citizens, children, and the poor. But if cost is our main concern, then the proposal to grant early release seems compelling. The prison system would save a considerable amount of the money now spent on medical care and security. Some prison officials, facing serious budgetary constraints, find the early-release programs attractive, but the issue of early release for AIDS patients is an explosive one. Some of the most liberal prison officials have fought for early release, believing that compassionate care for these individuals could be achieved by releasing them. Other prison officials simply want to dump the AIDS problem on the community even though many community agencies will not accept ex-convicts, and they often end up with no one to care for them.

Fortunately, some innovative programs for inmates infected with H.I.V. have been developed. The state of Rhode Island, with the help of Brown University, has a plan that provides AIDS education, H.I.V. testing and counseling, and—most important—follow-up services after release. Cooperative services drawn from the state health department, the state correctional department, and the university manage patients' care during incarceration and after release. Continuity in managing the care is the most significant factor. Inmates with H.I.V. who are about to be released are referred to community-based agencies for services. They are then often followed by the same team and the same doctors who treated them in prison.

This program is a model for what may be the best approach to managing the growing number of inmates who are H.I.V. positive or who have already developed AIDS. With its three-department team approach, it ensures that incarcerated inmates are given care, yet reduces the cost of that care by providing services inside the facilities instead of transporting the inmates to expensive off-site hospitals. In addition, this program helps to reduce the spread of AIDS in the community by working with the inmates after their release. Through intensive, ongoing AIDS education, the teams teach inmates how the disease is spread and emphasize the importance of protected sex and the dangers of sharing needles.

In the Bedford Hills Correctional Facility, in New York, a state prison for women, the ACE program was developed by the inmates for support and education about AIDS. The ACE program sets up a buddy system in which inmates accompany other inmates to medical appointments, and hold meetings to provide support and help for one another in dealing with the knowledge that they are infected with a deadly disease and may spend their last few years away from loved ones, and without freedom. Many are devastated by the fact that their children are dying of the same illness. The support of other women in the same predicament is often their only comfort. Away from their children, their days numbered, and often in great physical pain, this support is all they have.

The enormous increase in the prison population in the past ten years has taxed an already fragile system to the brink. The AIDS crisis is pressing that system even further. If we cannot accommodate the number of inmates sentenced to incarceration, and if most correctional institutions are overcrowded and forced to function well above capacity, how can the system also manage the problems of a large H.I.V.-infected population requiring intensive care and treatment, enormous resources, and a great deal of compassion? Only through creative, cooperative programs using the resources of the education, health, and correctional systems, can we attempt to find solutions and provide the humanitarian care, rehabilitation, and punishment that the correctional system is supposed to offer.

Chapter Six

It is difficult to imagine that in the twenty-four years since 1971, when President Richard Nixon declared a war on drugs, the United States has spent $70 billion on fighting drugs. Former New York City police commissioner Lee Brown observed in an interview quoted in *The New York Times,* "I look at the message coming from Washington that we are winning the war on drugs and I don't know what city they're talking about. It's certainly not New York City." Nor is it any other city in the country.

Since 1971, when the federal Drug Enforcement Agency was created, the drug problem in the country has changed, and so has the way we as a society have responded to it. Several states have passed laws pertaining to drug use. The laws reflect a wide range of approaches, from decriminalization of possession of small amounts of marijuana, to giving people traffic tickets for smoking the drug, to life sentences for possession of heroin.

In the 1970s the "drug problem" consisted of a large number of young people smoking marijuana and a group of heroin addicts who existed outside the mainstream of American society. In response, President Nixon spent $3 billion for treatment, education, and the development of methadone, a synthetic drug created to block the effects of heroin in the body.

Then in the 1980s cocaine and crack exploded into society. Cocaine—previously regarded as a "recreational drug" used by wealthy people—moved out into a larger sphere. Crack, the cheaper, smokable version of cocaine, invaded the streets, especially in poor neighborhoods. Drug-related crimes immediately skyrocketed. President George Bush spent $12 billion in 1991 on enforcing drug laws, on police training in South America (a major drug source), on placing drug agents at our national borders, and on jails and police officers. There was a major shift in funds away from education and treatment and into the arrest, conviction, and incarceration of drug offenders.[1]

Drugs and their impact are at the heart of some of the devastating issues the correctional system faces today. The explosion in drug use and the subsequent rise in violence have resulted in overflowing jails and prisons, with recidivism at an all-time high. A large number of Americans are dependent on drugs. Some of the substances they use cause chemical reactions that provoke violent behavior. They commit crimes to feed their habit, and their entire existence is centered around drugs and crime.

In 1986, according to the Bureau of Justice Statistics, 43 percent of state prison inmates had been using illegal drugs daily or nearly daily. Almost 20 percent were using "major drugs"—heroin, cocaine, methadone, or PCP (phencyclidine). About 35 percent of state prison inmates reported that they had been under the influence of drugs when they committed their last offense.[2] By 1991, 32 percent of inmates reported using cocaine or crack on a daily basis; 62 percent reported regular use of a drug.[3]

Earlier studies had shown that cocaine was used more than heroin, but the drug used most often during the time of an offense was marijuana. Drugs had become a part of these inmates' lives early on. Almost half of the state prison population started drug use by the age of fifteen, and followed a route from juvenile reform schools to institutions, jails, and repeated incarceration. By 1991, 50 percent of inmates aged seventeen or younger were drug users. Over all, about one-third had turned to crime to get money for drugs. About 30 percent of daily users of major drugs had six or more prior convictions.[4]

The Bureau of Justice Statistics conducted an intensive study of nearly 400,000 inmates held in over 3,000 jails. This study confirmed the drastic increase in drug use and its relationship to crime. It also reported an increase in the percentage of black inmates, from 35 percent to 48 percent. Hispanics increased from 20 to 25 percent, and women from 9 to 14 percent between 1983 and 1989. About 50 percent of the inmates held in local jails in 1989 had used cocaine or crack compared to 38 percent in 1983.[5]

Persons held in local jails accounted for 23 percent of all those held in 1989, and 9 percent of those in local jails were charged with drug offenses—possession, trafficking, importation—as their most serious charge. More than 70 percent of those in jail on drug charges had served at least one prior sentence of probation or incarceration. Of these drug users,

A very large percentage of young offenders are drug users, many turning to crime to get money for drugs.

one in six had been convicted of a violent crime such as robbery.⁶

When multiple charges against individuals were considered, the percentage of inmates with at least one drug charge rose from 11 to 26 percent. One in three women were charged with drug offenses, an almost sixfold increase from 1983. These increases are staggering. No one was prepared for the enormous impact of drugs on the criminal justice system, the courts, and the jails. How could we have prepared for an increase in drug arrests from 583,500 in 1983 to 1,247,800 in 1989, an increase of over 114 percent? In addition, an even more frightening increase occurred in drug arrests among women, from 79,800 to over 208,000. This has had a profound impact on a generation of children. The state now has the responsibility of raising thousands of children who have no homes, who lack parental love and care, and who may be afflicted with AIDS from a drug-addicted mother.

One can imagine the sense of hopelessness that corrections officials feel about this population, as almost 50 percent of convicted jail inmates who used drugs daily had previously participated in some type of drug treatment program. This clearly signals a failure to keep this population away from drugs and out of jail or prison.

This growing drug-addicted population is mostly African-American and Latino, with a decrease in white non-Hispanic inmates from 44 to 26 percent. Most inmates are young: roughly a third are between eighteen to twenty-four years of age, and more than half of those in jail in 1983 and in 1989 had not received high school diplomas. As the nation rapidly grows toward a highly technological society with more jobs requiring greater skills, this is a clear prescription for a life without hope or expectations. About 77 percent of the jail population had previously served time in jail, prison, or other correctional institutions, or had been sentenced to probation, and about a quarter of those charged with drug offenses had juvenile records.[7] Unfortunately, a juvenile record along with the lack of a high school education makes most inmates unemployable after their release.

José, Mary, and George are among thousands of inmates who fit the typical profile of those incarcerated for drug-related crimes. All three are in their twenties, started using drugs in their teens, used drugs regularly for about a year before their first arrest, and like 50 percent of the inmates held in local jails in 1989, used crack and other forms of cocaine. Like 30 percent of other jail inmates, they used the drug daily in the month before their arrest. Like over 50 percent of other jail inmates, they did not have high school diplomas and were serving less than nine months in jail—the average for half of the drug offenders. Those transferred to state prison for a felony charge, like armed robbery, serve much longer sentences—five years on the average. Like 77 percent of inmates in jail, all three of them had previous convictions. George and José both had juvenile records. Mary and George came from single-parent households, like 82 percent of those who used drugs. José fit into the 14 percent of inmates who had lived in foster homes. Among this group, 87 percent of the inmates had used drugs.[8]

By looking at this group, we can create a picture of a population that seems destined for incarceration. So many drug offenders fit into a similar pattern and have common characteristics: race, education, poverty level, family background, age at their first drug use, their choice of drug—cocaine or crack. Incarcerated crack users are likely to be black and female, under thirty years of age, and with no high school diploma. About 50 percent are unemployed. Like 39 percent of other crack or cocaine users, they commit crimes primarily to obtain money to buy drugs.

George, José, and Mary did not know each other on the streets, yet their stories are astonishingly similar. Mary got pregnant at sixteen. She ties the rest of her life to that event. She was a relatively good inner city student who began to lose interest in school and in life. She admits she had a caring mother who tried to support her four children without a husband. She remembers that her mother was sometimes employed and at other times was on public assistance. Although her mother warned her about running with the wrong crowd, she hung around with kids who lived on her block. Mary, looking many years older than her age, with deep, sunken eyes, never thought of herself as particularly pretty or outstanding. She didn't like to read or go to school, but she hoped to become a beautician. "What can I tell you?" she says, shrugging her shoulders. "I went out with this guy I knew, and it happened." To that casual statement she adds, "And the rest is history. I got pregnant. Like all other teenagers, I never thought it would happen to me. Somehow, when you're young, you don't really understand that if you go to bed with a boy, you'll probably get pregnant."

Like many other girls, she never thought about protection and would not have felt comfortable insisting that her boyfriend use a condom. She became pregnant after a few months of dating this friend, and by the time she found out that she was pregnant, she had stopped seeing him. "Did it ever occur to you to have an abortion?" I asked. She shook her head, signaling no.

She stopped going to school before the baby was born and stayed at home. Even though her mother helped her take care of her baby, who was born with numerous disabilities, she felt totally overwhelmed and at times wished the baby would die. She remembers going to clinics, unable to really comprehend that this baby would require a lifetime of medical care. She fell into a deep depression and began watching television all day.

Feeling isolated, and unable to care for her child, she started hanging out in the neighborhood at night. "Ironically, all the time that my mother was bugging me about hanging with the wrong people, I wasn't. I was just hanging out with one guy who got me pregnant. After the baby was born—with all the medical problems she had, my not going to school, having nothing to look forward to, and having few friends—I just snapped. My mother and I got into terrible fights about my not taking care of the baby. So I just sort of left, and I left the baby with her."

Feeling guilty and aimless, she moved in with a friend from the neighborhood and started smoking crack. "It was so easy. I just got into going to parties at night, hanging out with people who made me feel good about my life when, in reality, there was nothing to feel good about. Nothing in my life was working. I had a kid I could not deal with. My mother, already overwhelmed with her own kids, had to take care of my kid, too. I couldn't find a job. Actually, I didn't even know how to look for one. I really didn't know how to do anything but hang out with this group of neighborhood kids who were also going nowhere, running through life aimlessly. By the time I was seventeen, I was smoking crack regularly."

About the same time, her mother's apartment was burned out in an electrical fire. Her mother moved in with her sister, Mary's aunt, in another part of town. With three other children to support she had to put Mary's baby, who needed a great deal of special care, into a foster home.

"My mother tried everything. While she didn't know that I was dabbling in drugs, like everyone else in this group, and had a boyfriend who used drugs, she knew that I wasn't doing anything. But what could she really do?" Very quickly, in less than a year, Mary was craving crack and was on the streets selling her body to support her habit. Characteristically, crack addicts crave the drug all the time. Needing it often, they quickly become addicted. Cocaine escalates the user's craving. Users need more and more drugs for satisfaction. "You can't have just one," Mary says. The more they snort or smoke cocaine, the more they want. Coke takes over their lives, and the pursuit of more and more drugs is the only thing that matters.

Mary started to help some friends sell drugs in the neighborhood, and soon was busted for trying to burglarize an apartment with her boyfriend. Like 27 percent of drug users in jail, she was under the influence of drugs at the time of her arrest. Mary was arrested, after a year or two of regular drug use.

Now twenty-three years old, she has spent her adult life undergoing drug treatment. Like other drug offenders, she will need to go through several treatment cycles. She has been charged with several misdemeanors: prostitution, selling drugs in her neighborhood, small-time burglaries, stealing, and so on. From her first arrest to her current incarceration, she has spent less than a year in jail. Previously she pleaded guilty to lesser charges and went back on the streets to hustle. "I guess, I should be thankful that I have tested negative for H.I.V."

I asked her if she had any plans for when she is released from jail, in four months. "Sure, I want to get off this cycle. I want to get into some school. I want to get out of my area. But I am not going to lie—I want to, but I don't know if I will or if I can."

Many drug offenders in jail start attending classes, but most aren't incarcerated long enough to earn a high school diploma. After their release, they have no place to go except back where they came from, and they don't know how to find employment because they have never had a job.

José is not as lucky as Mary. He is infected with H.I.V. Like George and Mary, he started using drugs as a teenager. He came from a Latino family; both of his parents worked and provided a reasonable home environment. They gave him a strong religious background, and he went to church as a child.

José was a small child and looked delicate. "I always hated being picked on, teased, and beat up," he says. So he joined a gang, hoping they would protect him. Taking drugs was a necessary part of being a member of this group and receiving its protection. The members also hung out on the streets and got into trouble. "When my father found out that I hung around with some of these kids," José told me, "I got a real beating. He threatened to kill me if he found out that I continued to be a part of this gang." José's father did not fully realize how much difficulty his son had in the streets. If he wasn't with this group, he was often teased, hit, abused, and made fun of.

José says, "The pressure just got to me." That is his only explanation of why he started a life of drugs and crime. "I missed school a few days. My father came at me with the belt till I was bleeding." In many Latino families, a father feels that he has the right to beat his kids if he thinks that they've done something wrong. José became more and more dependent on his group, needing the sense of belonging. He found himself strongly influenced by some of the bigger boys. He started to fail subjects in school and to play hooky regularly.

"One night it just happened," he says. "We were all goofing around, jacking each other up, daring to do one thing or another. We took a car for a joyride, stole some money from a man who was just walking on the street by himself. Then we smoked some dope. When I got home my father wanted to throw me out, but my mother begged him to give me another chance. I got another chance. They said I could stay if I went to school, came straight home afterward, and studied. I wasn't allowed to play with the kids. My father had worked hard all his life to keep me off the streets, so he didn't want me doing anything except going to school and making something out of myself. Unfortunately, I was not a good student and I just lost interest in school. I hated going to classes, I was always embarrassed because I didn't do my homework and didn't know the answers to any of the questions. Within six months, I dropped out of school. I just couldn't tell that to my father."

José moved in with a cousin who earned money by stealing cars on order from a gang that sold the parts to used-car dealers. By the time José was seventeen, he was using drugs like many of the other teenagers around him. Within two years he was arrested, served a few months in jail, plea-bargained to a lesser charge, and was back out on the streets.

Now, ten years later, he has gone through the full cycle, like so many other drug users. He has tried to stop using drugs and has attended drug programs that worked for short periods of time. He could go home only if he was not using drugs, and for years he tried to avoid hurting his mother by not letting her see him while he was high on drugs. As an intravenous drug user, he used heroin and cocaine, smoked crack, and committed crimes daily to support his habit. Three years before this incarceration, he tested positive for H.I.V. "I was just beginning to take seriously the idea that I needed to stop using drugs because I still wanted to do something with my life. But then, after I found out that I was going to get AIDS and die, I really stopped caring. I committed more and more crimes. I got high as often as I could, and crack made me violent. I spent most of the last three years in jail waiting for trial or sentencing."

José is now waiting to be transferred to a state prison after being convicted on a robbery charge—the most serious offense in his ten years of living outside the law, using drugs, and committing crimes to support his habit. He can't bring himself to call home. "I just can't face my mother. I can't tell her to come visit me in jail because I am going to get AIDS and die."

George, now almost thirty, looks weary as he recalls living a life of drugs and crime from the time he was a teenager. Like Mary, José, and most others incarcerated for drug use, he has been in jail many times since his teenage days; he has spent as many years incarcerated as living on the street. He is as familiar with jail routine as he is with life on the outside. During this prison term, he learned new hustles from fellow convicts. The time in state prison was his longest period off drugs, and he finished his high school equivalency program behind bars. "Now, if I could just find a job, I would really quit the street life. I feel it."

George had enrolled in a drug program inside prison and seems more determined and optimistic

about leaving his troubled life behind. Like other drug offenders, he is finally tired of the life of drugs—the crimes, the jails, the police chases, the fear of contracting AIDS from intravenous drug use, and the fear of dying. George has had enough. He wants out. For him, as for many of those who truly want to get away from the life of drugs, crime, arrest, and prison, the hard road to change is just beginning.

Like AIDS, drugs—specifically cocaine and crack—have had a major impact on the problems confronting the correctional system in the 1980s and 1990s. About a third of the crack users were in prison for a violent offense and over a half had committed crimes to get money for drugs. The jails and prisons were flooded with drug offenders, while at the same time, during the Reagan administration, funding for many drug treatment programs was cut. Cocaine and crack addiction are even more difficult to treat than heroin addiction, and many of those using crack experienced violent episodes and soon found themselves needing more and more drugs to satisfy their habit. This craving led to more serious crimes and to further arrests, creating a need for space behind bars for these vast numbers of inmates. The system could not meet the need for drug treatment and drug education.

The prison population includes every conceivable high-risk group: those without high school educations, convicts without any skills, large numbers of blacks and Hispanics, many women with children, 77 percent with prior arrest records, and most of these

For prisoners who have spent years in the correctional system, life in the outside world seems frightening.

at risk of AIDS through intravenous drug use and prostitution. While 24 percent of the major drug users sought drug treatment, most participated in only one treatment program. Most of those were in treatment while serving time, but that is the time when they are least likely to use drugs, because they are away from the pressures that led them to use drugs.

For incarcerated drug users, the threat of AIDS is very real. As one drug counselor put it, "The fear of getting AIDS has a major impact. They either stop using drugs or do the opposite—totally give up trying to quit." Like the general population, African-Americans and Latinos were not really worried about AIDS in the early 1980s. It was seen as a gay disease. They gave little thought to the dangers in sharing needles, nor did they know how quickly the epidemic would spread among heterosexuals. They did not calculate the risks from drug addicts who often have multiple sex partners, from homosexual experiences in prison, and from female drug users who support their habit through prostitution. Some realized the high risk of AIDS, got scared, and stopped using drugs. Others, while not yet suffering with AIDS, were H.I.V. positive and knew that they would probably develop AIDS and die soon. Some of them decided, "Why bother quitting now? It's too late."

In addition to their lack of education and opportunity, their criminal records, and the looming menace of AIDS, many incarcerated drug users are overwhelmed by the enormous problems that develop through years of drug use. They cannot imagine how to transform their lives—how to work at a job or finish school, particularly at a time when the country is still feeling the effects of an economic recession, when people with skills, education, and no arrest records are competing with them for menial jobs that pay low wages. What is the likelihood of a black person with no skills, no education, and several arrests becoming an employed, taxpaying citizen? It seems hopeless. As a result, many of these drug users see no choice but to stay on the street, often homeless, or in jail and without hope.

Chapter Seven

Men in Prison

Each prison has characteristics of its own. Most older prisons are built of cement and concrete blocks that keep the noise level at the maximum. All the cellblocks open onto a corridor so that an officer can see into hundreds of cells at once. The bars are just far enough apart for inmates to extend their hands and, in some places, wide enough to pass food into the cells. In many prisons, all the areas are open for everyone to see. Toilets, showers, and beds are all in plain sight. Every few feet, there are doors that are locked and unlocked continually, and each corrections officer carries dozens of keys dangling on a chain. Movement through the corridors is usually slow, as officers must stop to open and then relock the steel doors.

Greenhaven, a maximum-security facility for men in upstate New York, is perched on hills outside a quiet community with small general stores that sell everything from hot dogs and newspapers to gas and batteries. Dairy farms spread over the surrounding area. Greenhaven is a vast, sprawling institution, with watchtowers that overlook the region. When you ar-

Greenhaven, a maximum security prison

rive, you know that you have reached a prison, even if you miss the sign that welcomes visitors.

Greenhaven houses over 2,000 inmates, including 1,100 lifers—those serving life sentences. This institution has the elements necessary for a prisoner to be able to settle in, to spend many years or even an entire life. Unlike jails, which house transient inmates, a maximum security facility has a settled, permanent feeling. Here, prison officials claim, they have the easiest time with inmates: few security problems or discipline problems, and, as Superintendent Charles Scully pointed out during our conversation, "The inmates don't want any problems." They want to do their time and be left alone. Prisoners want to know that the corrections officers are in control.[1]

The concrete blocks and cement walls of Greenhaven contain a community. As in other huge facilities, there are numerous buildings, many connected through underground tunnels. Some inmates are sleeping in their cells. Some are reading or sitting in the law library, but most are in the yard playing ball and enjoying a beautiful sunny day. For various activities, the prisoners move from one cellblock to another, stopping to wait for guards or, as they are now called, COs (corrections officers), to unlock the gates. Some teach or attend a class on anger resolution, others prepare food for dinner or work in the laundry or elsewhere. Many sit in solitary confinement. Prisons are a little like schools, with their populations divided into grades and grouped by level of ability for different subjects, and with honors classes and special classes for the disabled and for the athletically gifted.

Greenhaven also has a special psychiatric unit. It provides close supervision and daily medications for some inmates; others are in day programs for counseling. These inmates all stay in a separate environment to protect them from the rest of the inmates and to allow them to assemble their own peer group.

This institution has a separate cellblock for those on the prison honor roll—inmates who have had no infractions in two years. They often wait over a year to get into the program. The honors cellblock seems to look like heaven to the inmates, although to us, it seems like no place we would ever want to live. The inmates have bigger cells and can launder their own clothes in a washing machine on their own floor. The two television sets on the floor give them a choice of programs. These inmates can stay out later in the prison yard, too. Prison officials recognize that, as in school, management is based on control and discipline: rewards for good behavior, punishment for misbehavior.

The prison superintendent, like the mayor of a small town, worries about the school system, the hospital on the prison grounds, the psychiatric service, the recreational facilities, the meal schedules, and the general welfare of over 2,000 men, all dressed in the green pants and jackets worn by inmates.

In prison management a key factor is the age level of the inmate population. Younger inmates are more restless and cause greater discipline problems. They are not settled into prison life and to "doing a bid," as inmates refer to doing time. Older inmates have usually committed more serious crimes and have probably already served time in institutions. They know they are in prison for a long time. In most states the selection of the place where they are sent is used as a disciplinary measure. In New York, no one wants to serve in Attica, a place inmates dread because it is far away from the inner cities where many inmates come from. Also, most of the corrections officers at Attica are white, while over 85 percent of the

inmates are black or Hispanic. These guards earned a reputation for unusual cruelty and lack of sympathy during lengthy prison riots in the 1970s that resulted in the death of dozens of inmates. It's also bitterly cold in the area.

Generally, the long-term inmates try to stay out of trouble and do their chores. Most prisons are run, essentially, by the inmates, who have cleaning and maintenance assignments, or work in the kitchen or elsewhere. A few of the trusted ones and those with more education are able to land plum jobs in the offices. In short, the inmates take on the hundreds of functions necessary to the running of a facility. Men in prison look very fit because they spend many hours in the yards working out and lifting weights. They put their energy into physical activities.

Nevertheless, at Greenhaven, as in most prisons, inmates and staff agree that the inmates are idle too much of the time, and this idleness contributes to fights and disruptions. There used to be a prison car-repair industry, but it was eliminated due to a shortage of money. Some inmates prepare for factory work by punching a clock and working with machines, and some learn to make furniture, but these programs, like a number of others, accommodate only a few inmates. Superintendent Scully, after twelve years of presiding over Greenhaven, presents a picture of an orderly institution. He says that since the facility houses inmates for long periods, they are able to enter structured programs such as the high school equivalency program or the drug treatment program. Many prisoners are able to complete high school and then get a college education, even

The recreational yard at a men's prison

though they entered prison reading at a third grade level.

Most of the inmates here, and in other institutions across the country, were convicted of drug-related offenses, and often there are too few counselors to serve this population. However, here, as at other maximum security facilities, inmates serve for many years. Thus, they feel that if they have to wait a year or two to get into a program, there will still be plenty of time before they will leave the institution—if they ever will.

"The wave of the future," says Superintendent Scully "is peer counseling, where inmates will take over their own destiny," while still recognizing that they are under state supervision. This philosophy and approach to rehabilitation is demonstrated in the veterans' program that is functioning inside Greenhaven.

The inmate leading the program—the deputy commander, as he is called—gave me a detailed description of the program that he and several dozen other veterans operate. Classes in self-discipline, anger resolution, stress management, and self-improvement are conducted daily. The program's goal is to help veterans with the special problems they face, and to identify the circumstances that led them to commit a crime. Many veterans serving time for a serious crime are first offenders, and yet their crimes were violent. Many were convicted of killing someone. The deputy commander, like other inmates, acts as a counselor and receives prison wages (two to four dollars a day) for his work in running this program.

At our meeting, the deputy commander was pacing under a magnificent model of a helicopter made by an inmate; a map of Vietnam was hanging on the wall. This man managed to earn a college degree in prison and wants to get a master's degree in psychology. His knowledge of that subject was evident as we talked, He continued to pace with his arms behind his back, military style. "What's so special about veterans?" I wondered. The deputy commander told me one inmate's story of his service in Vietnam. He and a number of other soldiers arrived in a small village just as the villagers were preparing to cook some rice. As they arrived, a hand grenade blew up and killed his best friend. He fired on the villagers, not worrying about how many he killed or wounded. He just tried to get out alive. After he was discharged and came back to this country, he went into a neighborhood, smelled rice cooking, heard an explosion, and was so overwhelmed by a flashback that he shot an innocent person.

No one knows how many veterans kill again in civilian life. Of course most return home, readjust to civilian life, and continue their lives as productive citizens. But many veterans came back from Vietnam, with severe mental problems or drug and alcohol problems. They were unable to find work or find a place in society, and some snapped. This deputy commander, George, was a first offender. He committed a horrible crime in a moment of stress to protect his brother, and someone died. He is serving a minimum of twenty-five years to life.

This program, like several others run by inmates, sends out a signal for the future. If inmates want to deal with their problems, find out why they are incarcerated, and begin to take responsibility for their actions, these groups are there to help them and to prepare them to leave the institution. In addition to veterans' programs, some male institutions—particularly those near inner cities with large populations of African-Americans and Latinos—also have extensive programs run by American Black Muslims and by Sunni Muslims, followers of the religion practiced in

Black Muslims at a Pennsylvania state penitentiary describe how they used their prison earnings to build a prayer mosque.

Middle Eastern countries. Twenty years ago Black Muslims were often viewed as destructive and violent, but now many are deeply committed to educating inmates, improving their self-image and establishing discipline. Prison officials have come to believe that the Muslim programs play a valuable role in establishing order and discipline in institutions.

Muslim inmates account for 10 percent of the population in some prisons. They wear a yellow kuffe, or prayer cap, with the green prison garb, pray several times a day, go to classes, and help tutor other inmates. The law library, used by prisoners who wish to learn their rights or help their attorneys with legal briefs, is often occupied by Muslim inmates. To some observers, they are model prisoners, respectful and disciplined, working toward worthwhile goals and using their influence to reach other inmates. At Greenhaven, the Muslims help administer a prison release program. They help each other prepare for parole by talking about the steps they must take as they prepare to meet with the parole board. These steps include finishing their education, working at an assignment for a period of time, having no incidents charged against them, and participating in a drug or alcohol treatment program. By completing these steps they show that they are ready for life on the outside. Perhaps they could go into a supervised work-release program, working during the day and returning to the institution at night. Or they might go to a halfway house, where they would be supervised while working as productive members of society.

I was escorted throughout the facility, without restrictions, by the director of programs at Greenhaven, who has served in the prison system for well over a decade. He is clearly proud of the many programs that exist within this prison, especially because most of them are managed by the inmates themselves. Some inmates work as counselors. Others earn a few dollars each day for performing chores, attending school, participating in group therapy or drug counseling, or managing programs for other inmates. Prison officials are convinced that inmates who are motivated will participate in these programs and that the rest of the population will just do their time.

In the last decade new and much harsher sentencing guidelines were introduced. These new sentences are clearly not aimed at rehabilitation. At Greenhaven, half the inmates are serving life sentences; many others are serving much longer sentences than they would have been given in the past. Therefore, for most inmates, rehabilitation is not a goal. Because of this, prison officials are concerned simply with the orderly operation of the institution and with giving those inmates who may return to freedom an opportunity to address some of their serious problems—illiteracy, a need for self-discipline, and a lack of socialization.

Many women gain weight while incarcerated. This may be the first time in the women's adult lives that they have been drug-free, eating regularly, and getting some medical attention.

Because of the differences in their offenses and the difference between the sexes, men and women create very different prison environments. Women are less likely to be career criminals. Some are substance abusers whose crimes are related to their drug use. Others have killed a relative or close male friend and are serving many years for manslaughter. They are rarely convicted of premeditated murder or robbery. Women are less violent on the outside and less violent in prison. They rarely run drug gangs or conduct drug wars with violent, ongoing retaliations. They rarely commit repeated robberies or are arrested for carrying guns. Inside prison, they generally follow the rules. In contrast, men are always afraid of becoming victims of violence inside the institution. Rape is commonplace, so many join gangs or form group alliances for protection. The level of sexual activity is high. Men are frequently taken by force, and brutal sexual attacks are often used to gain power. Prison officials are reluctant to admit that this activity is rampant.

Violence in male facilities is not new. However, the longer sentences now imposed for felonies create new challenges for corrections officers. Since men are more likely to commit felonies punishable by long, mandatory sentences, the problem is more severe in male prisons. "What do you do to keep inmates who are serving very long sentences from violating rules and regulations, since they really have little to lose?" I wondered.

At a place like Greenhaven the promise of perks, or privileges, keeps some of the inmates on good behavior. If they have committed no infractions, they can ask for a family visit. They are then allowed to spend a few days on vacation with their families in a separate trailer on prison property. It takes years to become eligible for this program, however, and eligible inmates may spend months on the waiting list. Prisons use this as a reward for good behavior, and the inmates try hard to earn it. Greenhaven offers two other strong incentives for good behavior: the fear of being sent to Attica and the wish to be transferred to the honors block.

Along with granting privileges, the correctional system has begun to use peer influence as a tool for maintaining order. This works well in male facilities. Peer group counseling and peer group programs designed to prepare inmates for release, or for a parole-board hearing, are effective in prisons where there is clear leadership. The programs provide a structure within which the inmates can form groups based on their desire to be rehabilitated or to do a good bid—that is, serve time without disciplinary incidents or unacceptable behavior.

Every prison has some troublemakers who get into fights and create discipline problems. Their behavior often lands them in a special housing unit, where they are locked in for twenty-three hours a day of solitary confinement.

Among prisoners, the most notorious facilities are Leavenworth, Kansas, the oldest federal prison, and Marion, Illinois, where Mafia boss John Gotti was sent. These federal penitentiaries, filled with convicts serving long or life terms for murder or manslaughter, seem the most frightening, but they are also the ones with the most firmly established style and structure. The inmates know they will be there for a long time—most of them for life. They don't need to maintain their street reputations for being "bad," for being men not to be messed with. Many of them know, and almost accept, that they will never leave the institution, so they begin to see it almost as a home.

The long prison terms dictated by mandatory sentencing guidelines, the increase in violent crimes, the changing racial and ethnic makeup of the inmate population, and the overwhelming substance-abuse problems all play important parts in shaping today's American prison culture.

Chapter Eight

As mentioned, the Bureau of Justice Statistics reports that the number of state and federal prisoners in 1994 reached a record high of more than one million, an increase of almost 188 percent in a thirteen-year period. Prisons were operating at 18 to 29 percent above capacity. The term "at capacity" is based on the number of beds in a facility and the availability of food, supplies, hygiene facilities, and staff. The annual cost of keeping inmates incarcerated is now $40,000 to $100,000 for juveniles and $25,000 for adults, not counting costs of police time, court and legal expenses, and costs of prison construction, estimated at $100,000 for a single prison cell. The costs will continue to escalate.

The current rate of recidivism makes us wonder what we are accomplishing. In 1986 nearly two out of three released convicts were arrested for a new felony, or were charged with violating their supervision requirements. There were 5 million adults serving sentences for a conviction; 66 percent of these were on parole or probation, or were being supervised in the community.[1] With these high costs and discouraging figures, it is not surprising that we question the effectiveness of the correctional system and often judge it to be failing. Several new and perhaps radical ideas have been presented as alternatives. One suggestion is that the government should not be the sole operator of the correctional system. Clearly this is a novel idea. Taxpayers have generally assumed that government is responsible for public schools and hospitals, police, and the correctional system, all of which serve basic needs of society. But the correctional system is overwhelmed by problems: the growing number of youthful offenders incarcerated for more serious crimes; the increased number of drug offenders serving longer sentences; the spread of H.I.V. and AIDS (estimated to affect one in four inmates in jails in New York City); overcrowding leading to the use of prison barges anchored in the waterways of major cities and the housing of inmates in barracks. These problems beg for new solutions.

One possible (partial) solution is the establishment of private prisons—allowing private (for profit) correction companies to build and operate prisons. Since government seems to be failing in the corrections arena, perhaps private companies can do better; costing the taxpayers less, providing many jobs and opportunities for investment, and taking care of this unpleasant responsibility. We can imagine some of the efforts to find catchy names for the companies: Prison, Incorporated, Prisons Unlimited, Punishment for Profit. But after the joking stops, ethical questions remain. Shouldn't the government oversee the punishment of those convicted of offenses against society? Shouldn't our taxes be used to rehabilitate inmates and not to enrich business operators? There are more questions, too: Do we want felons on the street or behind bars? Do we concentrate on low-level drug peddlers or pursue big-time drug dealers? How do we solve the problem of overcrowding? What are the alternatives?

Let's look at the private-prison alternative. We cannot afford to continue to build more and more prisons. Since the 1980s the focus has been on placing more offenders behind bars. In response to public demand, federal sentencing guidelines have led to a much greater probability of imprisonment for a large number of crimes, and to longer terms. In 1990, about 74 percent of the defendants covered by the Sentencing Reform Act went to prison, compared to 52 percent of those sentenced before the law went into effect in 1986.[2] However, the prison overcrowding caused by the reform act forced many courts to resort to plea bargaining for lesser crimes in 89 percent of the cases where convictions were obtained. Early-release programs were encouraged, resulting in vast numbers of offenders serving periods of probation or parole in communities.

We had no prison space for these increased numbers. For those with a capitalist dream and some good business sense, the situation seemed to offer a perfect opportunity to fill a demand and earn a good profit. What better business than prisons? There was a growing need for prison space and also a growing market for providers of cheap labor. Taxpayers wanted tougher sentences; the prison population had doubled, but the public did not want the government to raise taxes. So, since the government expected to spend at least $5 billion on construction of new prisons between 1985 and 1990, enterprising real-estate brokers devised a lease-purchase program that seemed to offer an attractive package to investors and the public.[3] In these private deals, the capital for construction comes not from tax revenues, but from private offerings of bonds. The government leases the facilities from the corporation and then acquires the rights when the lease term expires.

This plan allows the government to get around voters' opposition to bonds to finance the construction of new prisons. Senator Alfonse D'Amato of New York sponsored legislation in 1984 to encourage this type of private construction deal that allows tax credits and other incentives for investors. The billion-dollar prison industry can be lucrative for finance brokers, architects, developers, banks, and construction companies. Some people in the real-estate business boast that these prisons are the only real-estate properties that can guarantee 100 percent occupancy. In addition to constructing the prisons, these private corporations also operate the facilities.

At first, these plans seem like a good idea. Since we have to house about a million inmates, we obviously need new space. In almost all states, private firms provide prisons with services ranging from job training to management consultation. So what's wrong with the privatization of a system that is under siege and overwhelmed by the number of people it must accommodate? These facilities can be lucrative for private investors and could also provide the government with alternatives to the warehousing of hundreds of thousands of inmates at a high cost.

The largest private operator is Corrections Corporation of America. This company operates detention centers for illegal immigrants for the Immigration and Naturalization Service. It also runs a drug treatment center for the Federal Bureau of Prisons. Private businesses charge the government less per prisoner than the cost at federally managed facilities. The companies can charge less because they are not restricted by labor union contracts and civil service guidelines, including hiring and promotional regulations, seniority, retirement, and pension obligations.

However, some citizens oppose the idea of corporations entering the business of punishment. They feel that the authority to deprive people of their constitutional freedom should be restricted to government. They argue that the right to punish should be left to the state. In response, private companies argue that they only execute punishments the courts have already authorized and that they merely provide services for inmates by feeding, clothing, and training them. But clearly, operating a correctional facility is not the same thing as managing a cookie factory or running a hotel, and it is easy for inmates to be punished unfairly or mistreated.

Another aspect of privatization that raises concern involves the question of making profits on the prisoners. A private company running a prison does not have to pay the inmates minimum wages. Consequently, prison labor can be used to produce products cheaply. For example, RCA Service Corporation operates Weaversville Intensive Treatment Unit, a facility for juvenile delinquents in Pennsylvania. In 1982, another private company, PRIDE (Prison Rehabilitation Industries and Diversified Enterprises), assumed control of prison printing operations. Their goal was to make prison industries more profitable. The work that prisoners perform for private industry makes the inmates into an asset instead of a liability. Some prisons are given contracts by private businesses to harvest cotton, soybeans, corn, or other crops. The prisoners are paid a few dollars an hour, and advocates of prison privatization argue that this is good for all involved. It reduces the expense of feeding and housing the offenders. Inmates no longer sit and watch television all day; there are fewer fights and improved morale. They perform a few prison chores, and also work at assigned tasks, and earn wages—even if the wages are lower than the government minimum standard. As an additional argument, some experts in the field of corrections claim that private prisons may be run more efficiently than government facilities. For the managing company, there is the opportunity to earn a profit.

In 1991, twenty-one states employed inmates in various prison projects. Their work grossed $18 million. Even some major corporations now hire inmates. For example, TWA installed telephones and computers in the Ventura School in California, an institution for juvenile offenders, and prisoners were employed as reservation agents. Aetna employs inmates in Connecticut to microfilm health claims. Other inmates grind eyeglass lenses. In one work-release program, inmates leave the institution during the day to work at removing asbestos from buildings, then return at night. From the prisoners' earnings, the management deducts room and board, family support, and victims' compensation.

The recidivism rate for those working in the program at the Ventura School was reduced drastically from 40 to 4 percent, but inmates are carefully picked to work in these projects, and those who are chosen are usually at low risk for recidivism. It's hard to know just how successful these programs really are because the people reporting on them tend to be influenced by their own attitudes when interpreting recidivism figures and other statistics.

Critics of privatization suggest that it is a modern form of slavery. Unions argue that prisons for profit take jobs away from union workers. Profit-making

Inmates work in a prison industries project.

prisons have an unfair advantage in competition with companies that pay minimum wages or higher, and therefore cannot produce goods at as low a price.

Some corrections officers and state employees charge that by privatizing prisons, the government abdicates its obligation to punish and sells that responsibility to the highest bidder. States abdicate their responsibility, and eventually the idea that punishment, restitution, and rehabilitation are all supposed to be part of one system is lost. Critics feel that these private institutions are not likely to emphasize rehabilitation by providing education and vocational training, but may instead exploit cheap labor for their own profit.

The private companies are ready with rebuttals for each attack. Some do provide training. In fact, they encourage training because they produce products that require skilled workers. Some also provide education as part of their contract with the government. In the recent conservative political climate, concern for prisoners' rights has probably lessened. Some citizens are more concerned with reducing costs than with the well-being of prisoners.

While some small private prisons house inmates in motels or other buildings that don't resemble prisons, others look like any traditional facility from the outside. Inside, however, there is an important difference: the inmates are likely to be working instead of watching television or sitting idle.

Privatization of prisons is not the only alternative proposed to relieve the overcrowding of jails and prisons. Although funding for drug treatment and counseling and therapy programs has been eliminated or severely cut, new alternative programs have appeared since the 1980s. House arrests for nonviolent offenders, and boot camp for juvenile offenders are two of these.

Offenders placed on house arrest—meaning they are not held in a prison but are not permitted to move outside a very limited area—wear an electronic ankle bracelet at all times to monitor their movements. The bracelet is monitored through a telephone, as if Big Brother were watching. Usually these offenders are in a parole or probation program. Some are restricted to their homes, others may go to work. They may seem to be leading normal lives, except for the fact that they really cannot go outside the area monitored by the electronic bracelet. The ankle bracelet sets off an alarm if the offender moves beyond the prescribed limits. Some newer devices use computerized telephones and videotelephones.

About 12,000 people are monitored by electronic bracelets, in response to the ever-growing need to find alternatives to incarceration.[4] While the program involves only a small number of people, if these 12,000 people were in prison, they would cost taxpayers at least $25,000 per inmate per year.

Shock incarceration or boot camp is usually reserved for young, male, first-time offenders, or nonviolent inmates, although some states are trying the approach with other groups. The programs consist of physically working inmates so hard that they have no time or energy to get into trouble. The programs include tough physical drills, rigorous exercise, and a heavy work load. The strict discipline used in military boot camps, or basic training camps, is the basic model for this approach.

Some of these programs can serve as alternatives to incarceration for the entire sentence, and may last from three to six months. In other situations, individuals can volunteer or be court mandated to partic-

A corrections worker checks an electronic monitor.

ipate after serving some time behind bars. The goal is to learn self-discipline, something many young drug offenders lack. They are then placed on probation if they can find a job.

These alternative programs began as experiments designed for a small number of offenders, and they make only a minor dent in the prison picture as a whole. However, these programs—particularly those that also provide counseling, education, and training—have been successful in reducing recidivism, as seen in a three-year follow-up period. Since the average recidivism rate three years after incarceration is over 60 percent, and among juveniles 75 percent, any reduction in that figure is an important accomplishment. In addition, many young drug offenders enjoy the programs, which are tough and rigorous, like army training. The offenders enjoy the thrill of exercising and building muscles.

Joel is a teenager in a nontraditional alternative program. At our meeting, he was sitting on the sofa in his living room at home in a New Jersey suburb. One hand was on the television remote control, scanning back and forth between MTV and other cable channels. He appeared to be a normal teenager wearing faded jeans and a cap facing backward, but he wasn't. He was awaiting trial for manslaughter. His electronic bracelet was not showing, but he knew that all his movements were monitored by the device. He was out on bail, but couldn't go anywhere. He couldn't see friends; he stayed home watching television, opening fresh bags of potato chips. We didn't talk about the crime he has been charged with—causing the accidental death of a friend. A jury will judge his responsibility for that. He was waiting for his trial to start so that he could find out what the future would bring.

Physical training exercises at an Illinois boot camp

Joel is one of a handful of youngsters who are monitored by an electronic bracelet. He waits at home, instead of in a jail cell, to be tried on a manslaughter charge that in his state can bring a minimum sentence of eight to fifteen years if he is found guilty. As a juvenile without any prior arrest record, he was eligible for this program, which saves taxpayers money by keeping people out of institutions. Further, if found innocent, he has been spared the agony and lifetime scars that incarceration is guaranteed to inflict.

"Do you ever think about escaping?" I asked. It must be a terrific temptation, particularly for a young person. He responded with some sophistication and a vague smile. "If I admit to that, that's a violation of the conditions for being out of the joint."

Of course he had thought about running away. And, having watched hundreds of hours of television programs about criminals and prisoners, he was scared. He created elaborate escape plans in his head. He bit his fingernails and hoped to put this incident behind him. But I could not help thinking about the other boy's parents, who had to cope with the death of their only child. How did they feel about Joel being home with his parents, watching television, being taught by tutors, suffering a slight inconvenience because his movements were limited?

New York City is now looking at this alternative more seriously. With 22,000 inmates, the city correctional system has to find alternatives for housing offenders. The electronic bracelet accomplishes nothing in regard to rehabilitation or training, but it does monitor offenders outside prison so that they don't commit new crimes. However, in New Jersey in April 1992, one inmate managed to remove the bracelet and fatally shot a friend. Another inmate failed to show up for drug counseling and stabbed a man while attending a barbecue. A few incidents like these could bring the project to a quick halt, because officials fear hostile publicity. Such incidents could also lead the public to believe these bracelets are just a quick way to ease prison overcrowding and not a useful alternative. Other critics are concerned about the rest of the support system. Are these offenders receiving less supervision from probation officers as well as less counseling? Will they eventually return to prison once the bracelets are removed? Others question whether electronic bracelets are really a form of punishment. As with boot camps and private prison programs, the inmates eligible for electronic bracelet programs are, for the most part, considered nonviolent and are not drug offenders.

As prison costs and the number of inmates continue to rise, the search will continue for other alternatives and new long-term solutions. The superintendent of one New York facility described the situation: "You cannot solve the prison problem until you solve the other problems in America: education, families headed by single females, poverty, unemployment, and drugs. If you're educated and can get a full-time job, then you cannot really use drugs and you don't need to steal. How many college-educated people with full-time jobs do you think we have incarcerated? Very, very few. And they are in there because they got greedy and committed some fraud to get more money. But they probably did not stick up a bank, steal your car radio, or sell two ounces of drugs."

Yes, few college-educated people with full-time jobs are incarcerated except for embezzlement, bribery, forgery, and fraud—but these white-collar crimes increased by 25 percent between 1983 and 1988.[5] This increase was partially due to the greater use of credit cards and computers, which opened up new criminal opportunities. A prison address is reserved mostly for the uneducated, the unskilled, the drug users, and the young. These new initiatives do offer ways to ease overcrowding and may also take some of the burden off the taxpayers, who are tired of being victimized twice—first by being robbed or assaulted and then by having to pay for it with their hard-earned dollars.

Chapter Nine

Prison Life Revisited

I remember my feelings when I visited a maximum-security prison for men more than ten years ago, for research for *Prison Life in America.* When I returned to the prison to prepare for this book, the same strong feelings of fear and lack of control over my life resurfaced, and I was only a visitor; I was free to leave.

In some ways prisons have stayed the same: the deafening noise; the scorching heat during the summer; the sea of men dressed in green, moving in unison, instantly distinguishable as inmates. Many of the cells look alike: a bed, a toilet, a sink, a dresser, and a few books, some have numerous pictures of women, some have photos of family members. Everything is close enough to be reached from the bed by the extension of an arm.

Many things have stayed the same in the past decade, but now an entire generation of inmates has grown up in prison. We became tough on crime during the 1980s and the probability of a convicted offender going to prison increased. The ratio of prison admissions to the number of serious crimes reported is now at record levels, as is the number of arrests for serious crimes.

New trends have developed in the past decade. In the 1970s and early 1980s the issue of capital punishment was hotly debated. In 1976 the Supreme Court ruled that the death penalty was constitutional, and by the early 1990s, 36 states had enacted laws that permitted the death penalty. Now, with public sentiment increasingly favoring harsh punishments, the issue seems settled (for a period, at least) and it is likely that more states will adopt death penalty legislation. Each year we have seen an increase in the number of people executed. These executions still receive media attention, but no longer routinely make headlines. A total of 226 executions have taken place since 1976.[1] About 2,716 prisoners have been sentenced to death and are awaiting the results of appeals. The majority of death row inmates, 55 percent, are in the South, with Texas and Florida, along with California, having the highest percentages. Fewer than 7 percent are held in New Jersey, Connecticut, and Pennsylvania.[2] Most of those on death row are men, all have been convicted of murder. Thirty-five women and nearly the same number of minors have been sentenced to die. Although most condemned prisoners are white, 40 percent are black, which is more than three times the percentage of blacks in the general population of this country. The remaining 8 percent includes Asians, Native Americans, and Hispanics.

Today the most critical issue for the correctional system, and for the rest of society, centers on the fact that over 5 million people are under its supervision. Furthermore, 1 in every 25 persons age twelve or older was the victim of a violent crime in 1992. From 1973 to 1991, 36.6 million people were injured as a result of violent crime.[3] With this evidence of mounting violence, it is possible to understand public sentiment that our attention should be shifted to the victims, and away from prisoners' rights, prison conditions, and the hardships of inmates waiting to be executed.

In many urban areas the public is now concerned about the overwhelmingly large number of drug-related offenses, and about the number of African-Americans in prison. The National Center on Institutions and Alternatives, an organization researching prison alternatives, reports that in the District of Columbia, 42 percent of the black male population between 18 and 35 was enmeshed in the criminal justice system: either in prison, on parole, on probation, or being sought by the police. As many as 70 percent of black males had been arrested by the time they were thirty-five years old. This number is considered valid for many other urban areas as well.

Another new and very alarming phenomenon is that the criminal justice system is becoming the home and permanent address for the addicted and the homeless, and for juveniles who have never had real homes. In a number of conversations, the corrections commissioner, the staff, and others serving this population all pointed out that prisons are where society sends those people it can't handle. "It's not that the criminal justice system has failed. It's the school system, the families, the social system—the entire framework of some communities that have failed." Some people suggest that we fail many of our children and then, instead of treating them, we punish them. Even though they are still at an age when

A counselor (right) at a women's prison works with two inmates to help them prepare for their future.

they could be rescued and have full and productive lives, they are turned over to a system that will hold them for a while and then release them, fully expecting them to return. And, sadly, about 80 percent do.

I ended the last book by asking prisoners how they would face the difficult road back. "What are you most afraid of?" I now asked an inmate who was getting ready for the day he had been waiting for, looking forward to, and praying for. "I am afraid of leaving here," he said quietly.

"The road back into society is harder than it was ten years ago," he remarked, as other inmates nodded and agreed. "We still face all the problems of changing our lives, staying off drugs, finding a job to pay the rent. We know how hard it is to find a job, especially one requiring only minimal skills." Some said that they don't even know how to act in society, and are comfortable only among street people and other prisoners.

The atmosphere at Lincoln Correctional Facility in New York City seems particularly upbeat. Lincoln is on a busy street on the edge of Harlem. When I visited ten years ago and again on this return visit, I marveled at the facility's beautiful view of Central Park. The individuals here have been released from prison but are in a work-release program, still under supervision. By maintaining a record of good behavior in prison, they became eligible for this program two years before completing their minimum sentences, thus reducing the time they had to spend behind bars. The chance, or hope, of being accepted for the work-release program gives inmates a reason to do the right thing, as they put it. The program also reduces the number of prisoners and the prison overcrowding that longer sentences cause.

At Lincoln, the program members must either have a job or find one within six weeks. If they fail to do so, they must return to a much-dreaded upstate facility. The men go out to work every day and come to Lincoln every night to sign the roll book, speak to the counselor, and leave a urine specimen to be tested for drug use. Some are permitted to live with their families, if a relative will take them in. The others live at the center, dormitory-style, behind locked doors at night.

The center bears little resemblance to a prison. The inmates can be given a great deal of latitude because, as they say in prison, "It's at the end of the line." Here, if they mess up, they will be sent back—all the way back to a prison with cells, chains and handcuffs, locked gates and sirens, to serve their full sentences.

This program seems like a dream alternative to incarceration. Once an inmate is employed and has a home residence, and has a parole board hearing scheduled within six months, he can go home at night and never have to stay in the facility. The individual must keep a job, stay off drugs, and observe all the regulations. In the program men can work and save money toward their final release. They learn about scheduling and making commitments, because they must get to work on time and check in on time. They have to give up part of their wages to pay for the administration of the program so that the taxpayers will not have to foot the entire bill for their rehabilitation.

"Do the inmates actually find work?" I asked the friendliest superintendent I met in my prison travels, Frank Headley, who has been in the criminal justice system for over twenty years and has seen it all. He still has a sense of humor and a laugh bigger than Eddie Murphy's. Headley said that many of them do find work, some with the help of Lincoln's job developer who has a list of companies willing to hire convicts—perhaps in order to earn community goodwill and some tax benefits. "They take jobs that years ago they would have turned up their noses at. Most will take anything." But still, among the few hundred men in the program, a few do go AWOL, or come back intoxicated, or turn in a "dirty" urine specimen—one with traces of drugs.

Why would some prisoners go through years of incarceration, finally get into an early-release program and, in the last stretch of the journey, sabotage the situation so that they are sent back to prison? Superintendent Headley and the other staff members understand this problem only too well. Some convicts are afraid to go back to the streets. They really can no longer live outside a prison setting. Others have no place to go except back to a neighborhood filled with drugs and despair. So they commit acts they know will lead to a return to prison.

Many of them know they are H.I.V. positive. While some find the spirit to keep going—to look for work, stay away from drugs, and return slowly to the community—others just give up, as if to say, "What for? I am going to die soon anyway."

The road back *is* harder now. The economy is worse, so finding and keeping a job is far more difficult. The general population is less sympathetic to inmates and people with criminal records. It is harder to find new places to live, away from old neighborhoods and old friends. Still, many of the work-release program members come back to Lincoln every night, buzzing with energy, resolved that this is their last stop, that they are never going back to prison.

"What made you decide that you will commit no more crimes?" I asked one of the men. "I tested negative for H.I.V. and I said to myself, 'If I get through this thing, I'll never shoot drugs again.' I want to live, man. I've seen too many men die in front of my eyes."

Throughout the country there are hundreds of programs that try to help inmates build a bridge

A parole officer (left) works with a parolee on problems of adjusting to life outside prison.

from the life they have known and must abandon, to a new life in which they can truly leave prison behind. However, we still have to learn to deal with those people who continue to commit crimes because they don't want to or cannot change. And there are also those who want to go back to prison, either because they are afraid to leave or because they no longer know how to live in the outside world.

During the last decade, many difficult problems have swelled to threaten society: homelessness, new levels of poverty, mentally ill people living without supervision, and more. In our schools, teachers worry about security guards and metal detectors for gun control. They must spend time talking about AIDS, drug abuse, safe sex, and child abuse; sometimes neglecting the teaching of reading or math. Corrections officials dedicated to rehabilitation are now dealing with inmates who need to be socialized in numerous ways. They need basic education and discipline, as well as help in learning how to live with others in a civilized society. The officials know that some inmates want to learn and change but that others will never be productive. They will continue to commit crimes and will return to prison to spend the rest of their lives incarcerated. Now corrections officials are concerned about the spread of tuberculosis through jails and prisons; about an AIDS epidemic, and about unforeseen new challenges. Private prisons will continue to grow as an industry, and other new ways to cut the costs of incarceration will be developed. And last but not least, we must continue to search for new solutions to the problem affecting all of our lives, the problem that will continue to influence the future success of this country: are the prisons there to punish inmates or to rehabilitate them, and at what cost to all of us?

Chapter Ten

Society's attitude toward people accused of committing crimes has changed radically over the last twenty years. There is general agreement that the old policies and approaches of the criminal justice system have failed. Crime rates have surged, and the costs of managing the system reached $30 billion in 1994. Over one million inmates are in prison, straining a system that is bursting at the seams. And the public wants solutions.

In the 1960s and 1970s, public attention was focused on prison reform, on the inhumanity of the death sentence, and on the need to rehabilitate prisoners. In the 1990s, the focus is on the need for the death penalty to protect society, and on creating laws that mandate tough sentences and that restrict parole.

Twenty years ago the public viewed prisoners as people who had committed crimes, but who could often be helped to become contributing members of society. They could be rehabilitated, and with counseling, education, and job training, they could perhaps be released to halfway houses from which they could be reintegrated into society. The Fortune Society and dozens of other organizations were defending the rights of prisoners, investigating their treatment, providing legal assistance, and developing alternative programs to incarceration. Today those are not the dominant public concerns or attitudes; the public is now more concerned with its own protection.

We have come full circle in our attitudes. Repeat offenders who seem absolutely resistant to rehabilitation have pushed even liberal public officials like former governer Mario Cuomo of New York to support the rising public demand for mandatory life sentences for all criminals convicted of three felonies—the "three strikes and you're in" laws. Even before enactment of "three strikes" laws, the federal and state governments were already building hundreds of new facilities to house the rising number of convicted offenders. Mandatory life-sentence laws will produce a new influx of inmates, who will have to be incarcerated for a lifetime.

From mandatory life sentences, the next logical focus for an angry, frustrated, and frightened public is capital punishment. People convicted of three felonies must serve the rest of their lives in prison—possibly forty or fifty years, as offenders are increasingly younger. To some people, capital punishment seems a better (and, they assume, cheaper) solution. Some people believe it is the only solution, citing the criminal justice system's failures. They point to felons committing crime after crime, and say we can no longer view these criminals as candidates for rehabilitation. Therefore we should devote our scarce resources to the law-abiding sectors of society. They say we must protect society and charge that perpetrators of bestial crimes deserve no mercy. Other critics of the system argue that instead of spending $100,000 a year to incarcerate young offenders, and then releasing them back into the drug-infested, violent environment that shaped them, we should incarcerate them for shorter periods and then spend money on aftercare, to help them make the transition from the prison back into society.

The public's demand for safety and the fear of crime and violence have become primary concerns. Capital punishment and mandatory life sentences are emotional reactions, from a society tired of living in constant fear. This sense of fear and the outrage at the failure of the system has caused the change in attitudes.

While the approach now seems to be focused on getting tough with criminals, we may find that this does not solve all problems. For example, there are very high costs involved in capital punishment, both in the trial procedure and in the appeals process. And studies have shown that capital punishment fails to deter criminals. Mandatory life sentences will mean even higher budgets. To keep criminals in prison for a lifetime will cost over $1 million per inmate. However, supporters argue that locked up or executed prisoners are not able to commit additional crimes. They believe that we must provide the public with a sense of justice and that life sentences and the death penalty are the only adequate punishments for taking another person's life. They feel that more police, a tougher stand on crime, longer sentences and restrictions on parole are the only workable approaches to create a safe society.

In our anger, we have lost sympathy for why or how teenagers get involved with drugs, or commit crimes. We have lost patience with young people who get caught up in crime, with children who drop out of school, and who lack education or job skills. We don't want to invest our money in programs to give inmates a second chance by providing education and job training, nor do we want to risk allowing them to rejoin society. We can only hope the new approaches will result in reduced crime and a safer society. We can only hope that they will not become vehicles for warehousing an entire population, who will live out their lives in prison—at our expense.

An Epilogue
It would be inaccurate to end this book with the impression that everything in the criminal justice system is hopeless. While it is true that the recidivism rate is very high, and that too many offenders remain in the crime cycle, some do succeed in finding a positive path and become productive members of society. We have seen some 1994 statistics showing that serious crime rates have been dropping in New York City and other urban centers. This drop may be due to several factors: larger police forces, more aggressive arrest policies, and longer sentences. After all, offenders behind bars can't commit new crimes. But some part of the drop may be credited to a percentage of offenders who have resolved that they will not stay trapped in the crime cycle and therefore have changed their life patterns.

Although many drug-treatment programs are facing cutbacks in funding, and some have even closed, the ones that remain are often filled to capacity, with extensive waiting lists. One counselor observed: "Many of the people we are seeing are ready to break the habit. They want to stop using drugs, want to end their life of crime. Some have lost everything. They have served a number of jail terms; they're homeless and ill. They're scared and will take any job. Now the challenge is to find jobs, so they don't become desperate and return to drugs and alcohol, and to crime." Many have seen their friends die of AIDS, from bullets, and from drugs. Now they want to change their lives.

Kenny, a thirty-five-year-old man, seemed typical of the offenders stuck in the crime cycle—yet he gave me a sense of hope. He'd been a poor student, and lacked education and marketable skills. Hanging out on the streets, he learned to be a petty thief, advanced to street-level drug dealing, became addicted to crack and introduced his girlfriend to it, too (she died of AIDS), and served several sentences for drug-related crimes.

"I was released from Riker's Island [a New York City jail] the last time I served. For the first time, I didn't go home. I didn't see any of my friends, didn't check in with the dope dealer, or stop by a girlfriend's place. I made one phone call—to a drug-treatment program." He had been through a prison treatment program earlier, so I wondered what had changed. "I changed, I changed! I couldn't do it anymore. I could not go through that cycle again, knowing the end is always the same—either you go to prison, or you die."

Kenny completed a residential drug-treatment program and found a full-time job at minimum wages, working in a restaurant. It is the first job he has kept for longer than a year, and he has begun to see the children he left behind while in prison. "Are you happy now?" I asked. "No. I have a way to go. I don't like my job. I have very little money, but I'm not on the streets. I have some pride and I can enjoy my children. I'm grateful I am alive. Now, I have to do something with my life." That sentiment is echoed by many who want to make a change. They know they face a tough road back but are ready to tackle it. As a society, hopefully, we will give those who are deserving the opportunity to become part of a productive society.

Introduction
1. U.S. Department of Justice, Bureau of Justice Statistics, "State and Federal Prison Population Tops 1 Million," October 1994, p. 1.
2. Bureau of Justice Statistics, "Violent Crime in the United States," p. 2.
3. Bureau of Justice Statistics, "International Crime Rates," pp. 1, 2.
4. Bureau of Justice Statistics, "Prisoners in 1993," p. 1.
5. Bureau of Justice Statistics, "Criminal Victimization in the United States," 1992.

Chapter One
Reprinted from Anna Kosof, *Prison Life in America* (New York: Franklin Watts, 1984).

Chapter Two
1. Department of Justice Press Release, 1994.
2. Bureau of Justice Statistics, "Women in Prison," 1991, p. 1.
3. Bureau of Justice Statistics Special Report, Allen J. Beck, "Profile of Jail Inmates, 1989," p. 1. Survey of State Prison Inmates, 1991, p. 4.

4. Bureau of Justice Statistics, Department of Justice Advance Press Release, September 1994, p. 1.
5. Bureau of Justice Statistics, Patrick A. Langan, "Recidivism of Felons on Probation, 1986–1989," pp. 1, 5.

Chapter Three
1. Bureau of Justice Statistics, Allen J. Beck, Susan Kline, and Lawrence Greenfield, "Survey of Youth in Custody, 1987," p. 1.
2. Ibid., p. 2.
3. Ibid., p. 3.
4. Joseph Treaster, "Hard Time for Hard Youths: A Battle Producing Few Winners, *New York Times*, December 28, 1994, A12.
5. Bureau of Justice Statistics, Beck, Kline, and Greenfield, "Survey of Youth in Custody, 1987," p. 2.
6. Ibid., p. 3.
7. Ibid., p. 4.
8. Katherine McFate and Cheryl Reed, "Prisoners of the Drug War," *Focus*, May 1992, pp. 5, 6.
9. John Wilson, Jr., "High Risk Homes and Educational Failure," *Focus*, May 1992, p. 7.
10. Bureau of Justice Statistics, Beck, Kline, and Greenfield, p. 1; McFate and Reed, p. 6.
11. Bureau of Justice Statistics, Beck, Kline and Greenfield, p. 5, and Mandatory Sentence Guidelines.
12. Bureau of Justice Statistics, "Young Black Male Victims," December 1994, p. 2.
13. Bureau of Justice Statistics, Lawrence Greenfield, "Capital Punishment 1990," pp. 1, 7; "The Ultimate Price," *Scholastic*, April 5, 1991, p. 13.

Chapter Four
1. Statistics and figures presented in this chapter are based on: Bureau of Justice Statistics, Lawrence

A. Greenfield and Stephanie Minor-Harper, "Women in Prison," p. 1, 2, 4, 6.

Chapter Five
1. Joseph B. Treaster, "20 Years of War on Drugs, and No Victory Yet," *New York Times,* June 14, 1992, E7.
2. Theodore M. Hammett and Andrea Daugherty, "1990 Update: AIDS in Correctional Facilities," National Institute of Justice, July 1991.
3. Ibid.
4. Bureau of Justice Statistics Special Report, 1993.
   Additional sources:
   New York City Department of Corrections, personal conversations; *New York Times,* "Changes Expected with New Prison Cheif," April 20, 1992, B3; Personal conversations with incarcerated women.

Chapter Six
1. Joseph B. Treaster, "20 Years of War on Drugs, and No Victory Yet," *New York Times,* June 14, 1992, E7.
2. Bureau of Justice Statistics, Charles A. Innes, "Drug Use and Crime," State Prison Inmate Survey, 1986, p. 1.
3. Bureau of Justice Statistics, Survey of State Prison Inmates, 1991, p. 21.
4. Ibid., p. 4, 5.
5. Ibid., p.22.
6. Department of Justice, Caroline Wolf Harlow, "Drugs and Jail Inmates, 1989," p. 1.
7. Department of Justice, "Correctional Populations in the United States," 1991, p. 8.

Chapter Seven
1. Personal conversation with the superintendent.

Chapter Eight
1. Bureau of Justice Statistics, Louis Jankowski, "Probation and Parole, 1990," p.1; U.S. Department of Justice, "Probation and Parole Populations Reach New Highs," Advance Press Release, September 1994.
2. "Sentencing Law Jails More Federal Offenders," *Star Ledger*, June 22, 1992, p. 2.
3. Craig Becker and Amy Stanley, "The Downside of Private Prisons," *The Nation*, June 15, 1985, p. 728.
4. Charles Strum, "Fearing Felons on the Loose," *New York Times*, June 7, 1992, p. 31.
5. Jacob Perez, "Forgery and Fraud Related Offenses in Six States, 1983–88," Bureau of Justice Statistics, p. 1.

Chapter Nine
1. Bureau of Justice Statistics, Lawrence Greenfield, "Capital Punishment, 1990," p. 1, 2.
2. Bureau of Justice Statistics, "Violent Crime in the United States," p. 7.
3. Bureau of Justice Statistics, "Highlights from Twenty Years of Surveying Crime Victims, 1973–1992," pp. 6, 9.
Additional sources:
U.S. Department of Justice, Patsy A. Klaus, "The Costs of Crime to Victims," 1992, p. 1. Bureau of Justice Statistics, Darrell K. Gilliard and Allen Beck, "Prisoners in 1993," p. 9.

For Further Reading

Bender, David L., and Leone Bruno, eds. *America's Prisons: Opposing Viewpoints.* San Diego: Greenhaven Press, Inc. 1991.

DiIulio, John J. *No Escape: The Future of American Corrections.* New York, Basic Books, 1991.

Landau, Elaine. *Teens and the Death Penalty.* Hillside, NJ: Enslow, 1992.

Nardo, Don. *Death Penalty.* San Diego: Lucent Books, 1992.

Tucker, Julie N., and Barbara H. Olsson, eds. *The American Prison: From the Beginning . . . A Pictorial History.* Laurel, MD: The American Correctional Asso., 1983.

Warburton, Lois. *Prisons.* San Diego: Lucent Books, 1993.

Weiss, Ann E. *Prisons: A System in Trouble.* Hillside, NJ: Enslow, 1988.

Wicker, Tom. *A Time to Die.* New York: Quadrangle Books/The New York Times Book Co., 1975

Index

Note: Page numbers in *italics* indicate illustrations.

ACE program, 76
Aetna, employment of inmates by, 112
African-Americans: dropouts, 44; and drugs, 41–43, 80, 82; and H.I.V., 73; and homicide, 45–46; as I.V. users, 69; Muslim inmates, 101, *102*; and prison, 8–9; young, and crime, 43–44
Aftercare, prison, 133
AIDS, 12, 50; among homosexuals, 92; among inmates, 68; statistics in Canada, 69
AIDS inmates: and other prisoners, 69–71; rights of, 71; statistics on, 72–73; variety of, 73
AIDS treatment, cost of, 71
American Black Muslim inmates, 101, *102*
AZT treatment, 71, 73, 74

Babies: with AIDS, 82; with inmate mothers, 53–56, *55*
Baby boom, 24–25
Bedford Hills Correctional Facility, 76
Boot camps, 116–17, *118*
Brown, Lee, 78
Bureau of Justice statistics, 31, 35, 50, 79–80, 107
Bush, George, 26, 79

Capital punishment, 27, 123
CASAT (Comprehensive Alcohol, Substance Abuse Treatment), 53–54
Centers for Disease Control and Prevention, 45, 68–69
Cocaine, 79, 86, 91

Confinement, early, 19–20
Convict ships, 20–22
Correctional institution, for youth, *36*, 37, 39–41
Correctional system, impact of drugs on, 91
Correction officers, new problems facing, 130
Corrections Corporation of America, 110
Courts, early, 19–20
Crack, 66–67, 79, 86, 91
Crime: cost of, 14, 45; impact of, 15–17; statistics, 14, 28, 123; in urban areas, 124; and youthful offenders, 35–37
Criminal justice system, crisis in, 27–28
Criminals, society's attitude toward, 131
Cuomo, Mario, 132

D'Amato, Alphonse, 110
Deaths, drug-related, 45
Death sentences, among states, 123
Deportation laws, 20
"Doing a bid," 97
Dropouts, 44
Drug addicts, and AIDS, 67
Drug-related offenses, 30
Drugs: and criminal justice system, 82; and incarceration, 78–93, *81*
Drug use, among inmates, 74–75
Drug user profiles: George, 89–91; José, 87–89; Mary, 83–87

Drug war, cost of, 78, 79
Dueling, 20
Dukakis, Michael, 26

Early-release program, 61, 75, 109
Education: and crime, 43; and drug users, 83; and prison, 8, 120–21; and women prisoners, 51; and young offenders, 37
Electronic bracelets, 115, *116*, 117–20
Environment, and crime, *52*

Federal Bureau of Prisons, 110
Federal Drug Enforcement Agency, 78
Felons, 31
Fortune Society, 132

Gang influences, 87
Gladwin, Bridget, 49, 52–53, 60, 61
Good behavior, 105
Great Depression, 24
Greenhaven, 94–100, *95*, *98*, 103, 105

H.I.V., 12, 50, 59, 67
Halfway houses, 63, 103
Headley, Frank, 127–28
Heroin, 78–79
High school equivalency program, 89, 99
Hispanics (Latinos): and drugs, 41–43, 80, 82; and H.I.V., 73; as I.V. users, 69; and prison, 8; young, and crime, 43

Homicide, 14, 45–46, 50
Honors cellblock, 97, 105
Horton, Willie, 26, 27, 33
House arrests, 114–15

Illiteracy, 104
Illness, in prisons, 99
Immigration and Naturalization Service, 110
Inmates: activities of male, 96–97; as counselors, 104

Jail, 7, 8, *29*–30

Latinos. *See* Hispanics
Lease-purchase program, 109–10
Leavenworth Prison, 106
Lifers, 96
Lincoln Correctional Facility, 126

Mandatory life-sentence laws, 132, 133
Mandatory sentencing guides, 106
Marijuana, 78–79
Marion Prison, 106
Methadone, 79
Mothers, inmates, 53–56, *55*

National Center for Education Statistics, 44
National Center on Institutions and Alternatives, 124
National Crime Survey, 14
National Crime Victimization Survey, 17
National Drug Control Policy, 44
New York Times, 78
Nixon, Richard, 78

Parole board, 103
PCP (phencyclidine), 79
Plato, 19–20
Plea bargaining, 33–34, 109
Poverty, 12, 43
PRIDE (Prison Rehabilitation Industries and Diversified Enterprises), 111
Prison(s): cost of, 17–18, 107; counseling, *125, 129*; early American, 22; early Greek, 20; exterior, *10, 99*; interior, *16, 70*; library in, *113*; overcrowding in, 67–68; physical description of, 94–96, 122; private, 20, 108; profit-making, 113–15; security techniques of, *23*; statistics, 7–9, 13, 15, 22–24, 28, 30, 50, 51, 107; statistics for women, 50
Prison environments, men's vs. women's, 104
Prison Life in America (Kosof), 12, 122
Prison wages, 100, 104, 111–12
Probation, 30, 32
Providence House, 56–58, *57*
Public safety, 32–33, 133
Punishment, kinds of, 19

Rape, 14, 105

RCA Service Corporation, 111
Reagan administration, 91
Recidivism, 8, 9, 31, 32, 34, 51, 55, 107, 234; and alternative programs, 117; and drugs, 79; and work-release inmates, 112
"Recreational drugs," 79
Rehabilitation, 9, 60, 104
Rhode Island-Brown University, AIDS program of, 75–76

Scully, Charles, 96, 99, 100
Self-esteem, 63
Sentencing guidelines, 104
Sentencing Reform Act, 109
Sexual activity, among inmates, 74–75, 105
Single-parent households, and crime, 43
Stocks, *21*

Taconic Correctional Facility, *48*, 52, *55*
Teenage unemployment, 68

Television, crime programs of, 26
"Three strikes" law, 132
Tuberculosis (TB), 66, 73
TWA, employment of inmates by, 112

Veterans' program, in prisons, 100–101
Victim restitution, 31

Weaversville Intensive Treatment Unit, 111
White-collar crimes, 121
Women: drug-using inmates, 80; and homicide, 50–51; as I.V. users, 69; in prison, 13, 28
"Women in Prison" (Bureau of Justice), 50
Women's prison: interior, *62*
Work-release program, 61, 63, 126
Work therapy, 22
World War II, 24